W9-BCT-874

PLANNING EDUCATIONAL FACILITIES

Donald G.
MacKenzie
**Florida Atlantic
University**

UNIVERSITY
PRESS OF
AMERICA

Lanham • New York • London

Copyright © 1989 by

University Press of America,® Inc.

4720 Boston Way
Lanham, MD 20706

3 Henrietta Street
London WC2E 8LU England

British Cataloging in Publication Information Available

Library of Congress Cataloging-in-Publication Data

Mackenzie, Donald G., 1936–
Planning educational facilities / Donald G. Mackenzie.
p.   cm.
Includes index.
1. School facilities—United States—Planning.   2. School facilities—Extended
use—United States—Planning.   I. Title.
LB3218.A1M18   1989   371.6'2'0973—dc20   89–14610 CIP

ISBN 0–8191–7479–3 (alk. paper)
ISBN 0–8191–7480–7 (pbk.: alk. paper)

All University Press of America books are produced on acid-free paper.
The paper used in this publication meets the minimum requirements of American
National Standard for Information Sciences—Permanence of Paper for Printed Library
Materials, ANSI Z39.48–1984.   ∞

DEDICATION

This book is dedicated to those who want to build educational centers for everyone to use, and to the citizens whose taxes pay for school construction, and who should be allowed inside the schoolhouse.

ACKNOWLEDGMENTS

I wish to thank Dr. Charles E. Chick, retired Associate Commissioner, Office of Educational Facilities, State of Florida, and Dr. Paul Phillips, Associate Superintendent, Facilities and Operations, St. Lucie County Public Schools, Florida, for their review of the text and many helpful suggestions.

I also thank my wife Connie, who played a major editorial and support role in the writing of this text.

TABLE OF CONTENTS

Acknowledgments

Preface   ix

Introduction   xi

1. **Planning Process**   1

    Schooling and Education   2
    The Educative Community   3
    Rationale   4
    Community Education   6
    The Planning Process   7
    Planning Phase Components   8

2. **Beginning With Function Rather Than Form**   15

    Philosophies of Education   17
    Essentialism   18
    Perennialism   19
    Progressivism   20
    Existentialism   20
    Implications for Building Design   21
    Learning/Teaching Strategies   22
    Characteristics of Various Learners   24
    Preschool and Kindergarten, Ages 3-6   25
    Primary Grades, Ages 6-9   26
    Upper Elementary, Ages 9-12   26
    Junior High, Ages 12-15   26
    Senior High, Ages 15-18   27
    The Adult Learner   27
    Learning and the Older Adult   28

3. **Meeting Community Needs**   29

    Getting Started   29
    Step One: Orientation   30
    Step Two: Sensing General Interests   31
    Step Three: Looking for Partners   31
    Step Four: A Specific Plan   32
    Step Five: Existing Data   32
    Step Six: New Data   33
    Step Seven: Translating Data Into Needs   34
    Step Eight: Translating Needs Into Programs   35
    Step Nine: Determining Existing Facilities   35
    Step Ten: Establishing Building Requirements   35
    Step Eleven: Financial Resources   36

4. **Energy Use Considerations**   39

       Energy-Efficient Facility Design   39
       An Energy Conservation Program   44

5. **Vandalism Design Considerations**   47

       Defining Vandalism   48
       Social Considerations   50
       Physical Design Considerations   51

6. **Technology**   55

       Hardware, People, and Environment   55
       The Planning Process   57
       Technical Considerations   58
       Microcomputers   59
       The Management Process   60

7. **Resources**   65

       Chapter 1   Planning Process   65
       Chapter 2   Beginning With Function Rather
                    Than Form   68
       Chapter 3   Meeting Community Needs   68
       Chapter 4   Energy Use Considerations   69
       Chapter 5   Vandalism Design Considerations   69
       Chapter 6   Technology   70

       Appendix A   Community Dilemma   73

       Appendix B   Translating Needs to Design Con-
                         siderations   79

       Appendix C   Building Energy Survey Form   83

       Index   87

PREFACE

This is a book about <u>planning</u> educational facilities. But it is not the usual planning process associated with school construction. The planning process described in this text is meant to take place well before the usual school construction planning process begins.

The usual planning process includes such activities as selecting an architect, determining state-mandated educational specifications, or monitoring the various phases of construction. This process results in the construction of a school suited for young learners. I hope America will build no more such "schools."

We need <u>educational</u> <u>facilities</u>--places that will provide local citizens with educational services that are not being offered elsewhere. This means a facility where children might attend the traditional kindergarten through sixth grade classes. It might be where high school students attend the traditional high school. But in both cases, it could also be a place where pre-schoolers, elder Americans and non-traditional students could spend time in pursuit of learning.

Developing and planning an educational facility also means determining the various educational needs of the community, not just the schooling needs of children. This kind of needs assessment, plus a process that involves the community in the planning, will help to ensure a facility that will be fully utilized by the public from the very beginning.

Providing the community with an educational facility is so much more efficient and effective than using a building part-time just for children, or constructing many buildings, each at its own site, for community organizations that want to provide educational services. Instead of a school that serves a select population, for only part of the day or part of the year, a multi-purpose, educational facility could provide space for many of the educational activities for the entire community all year, day and night.

INTRODUCTION

Not many books have been written about school construction. Those books that exist usually discuss subjects such as the history of school construction, determining student populations, bidding procedures, how to select an architect, and the construction phase of the building project.

This text attempts a different approach. It suggests that what we need are not more school buildings. Instead, we need educational facilities-- ones that attempt to meet a variety of educational needs of the community. A school is a learning place usually designed for children and youth. Why not design a facility, not only as a learning place for children, but also to meet the other educational, physical, and cultural needs of the community. These needs can be met by having activities such as recreational programs, continuing education for adults, art exhibits, or musical and theatrical presentations. If a community needs courses or programs for college-age students, why can't that be included in the "school" design?

Each community is different--each has its unique educational needs. This assumption demands that every school be designed to meet specific local educational needs. Chapters 1, 2 and 3 discuss how this can be accomplished.

The remaining chapters examine three critical issues: (1) designing energy-efficient buildings; (2) incorporating design strategies to reduce vandalism; and (3) planning for the use of educational technology in the educational facility. These last chapters are designed to provide planning committees with sufficient information so they may raise questions about these issues with the architect. The success of energy conservation, vandalism prevention, and use of computers and telecommunications is more the result of strong community understanding and support than a function of architectural design.

The final chapter contains information on how to obtain additional resources for the planning committee.

Once the planning steps have been completed as outlined in this text, the organization can proceed with its standard procedure for construction of facilities. If the building program is developed without including these planning steps, there is little likelihood of developing anything but the traditional one-purpose school facility. No community can afford such inefficient construction and facility use.

When the school board decides either to build a new school or to renovate an old one, an attempt should be made to develop a facility that would house, at one location, several of the community's different educational programs. The decision to house these programs at one site must have a rationale that can easily be communicated to the public. This rationale springs from the concept of Community Education. Community educators attempt to bring into the traditional schooling process, local citizens and social agencies for a joint, cooperative and coordinated effort to provide better educational opportunities for everyone in the neighborhood or community. In Chapter 1, the rationale and concept are discussed and a planning process suggested.

The planning process details the steps needed for developing an educational facility rather than a school. It stops short of the traditional planning associated with public school construction and the steps needed to gain state department of education approval. These planning steps are well known by school plant planners and vary from state to state; therefore, they are not detailed in this text. In addition, while the school board may be the organization best equipped to provide much of the overall organizational expertise and financing, it should not be the only organization in the community to be involved in these activities. Other governmental units (county/parish government, community colleges, cities) have considerable expertise and resources and could provide additional administrative assistance.

In Chapter 2, philosophies of education are discussed. Although many may wish to avoid philosophical discussions, such discussions are vital to the process of determining the kind of building to be constructed and the justification for that building. If these basic matters are not resolved, trouble may be encountered late in the planning or building process.

This chapter also talks about learning theory as it applies to children, youth and adults. Philosophies of education and learning theories each have implications in the final design of the building.

Chapter 3 is intended to help the reader determine who ultimately will be the users of the educational facility. Discovering who the users will be (in terms of distance from home/work to the educational facility), will help determine who might help in planning, and those who should be contacted to determine community needs.

Once the planners determine which residents will probably use the facility, it is time to start gathering resources. These resources include brain power for current planning, future possible financial resources, and the utilization of other existing physical facilities that should be considered when planning for the development of this educational facility. The process should result in a plan for a coordinated educational facility for the community.

Chapter 4 concerns energy conservation--both passive and active. The success of some of the conservation measures suggested depends on community involvement and the development of a sense of community ownership of the facility.

Chapter 5 explores the prevention of vandalism. The chapter begins with some definitions, then briefly discusses social prevention strategies. Although most of the chapter discusses ideas designed to discourage vandalism, ideas will be of little help if the community does not feel the facility has been built for them. Without community support for the facility, vandalism cannot be stopped.

Chapter 6 discusses technological ideas as they apply to teaching and organizational telecommunications. Because of the basic and special wiring required, as well as the unique space needs for this technology, the equipment and space requirements must be considered early in the planning process. The inclusion of such technology in the facility holds promise for more community and agency involvement.

When the above special planning has been accomplished, traditional planning can begin for purchase of the site, selection of an architect, determination of a contractor, and the many other tasks involved. Many professionals and experts are available to assist with these tasks.

As the reader may have discerned by now, this text is following the very old precept: Form Follows Function. Many educational facilities are designed in the reverse order--that is, the activities (function) of an organization must adjust or adapt to an existing plan (form) or facility. While the financial saving may be considerable when we design form first, we may do a disservice to the community by using such plans. We may force neighborhood citizens to settle for a facility that only partially meets their needs. By failing to determine function first, and not implementing the concept of Community Education, we may save money and time but will probably not provide the community with the facility it needs and deserves. The author hopes that this text can play some part in convincing facility planners to involve the community when planning an educational facility and to design that facility to meet their needs.

CHAPTER 1

PLANNING PROCESS

Schools should be more than learning sites for children and youth--that is the basic assumption underlying this book. Spending ten or fifteen million tax dollars and devoting hundreds of hours of planning to develop a single-purpose building does not take advantage of the opportunity to develop a more functional facility. In addition, citizens are not involved in a planning and implementing activity that could serve to promote a greater sense of community among them.

The traditional school is planned for the schooling needs of children or youth. Meanwhile other educational needs of the community, including additional recreational activities, library services, community meeting rooms, expanded theatrical productions or preventative health services are probably being addressed by other organizations. Can the combination of the educational needs of the community with the schooling needs of children result in a more effective or more efficient delivery of services?

Both sets of needs are educational. Clearly children and youth primarily need specific and direct teaching/learning experiences--schooling. At the same time certain community needs such as health and library services are met by agencies which have at least a secondary educational function. Recreational services include teaching new skills or attitudes about winning and losing. Libraries are also involved in helping all community members learn. This is also true of the theatre or health organizations. While these activities/organizations are not _primarily_ involved in learning/teaching activities, they do have them as _secondary_ functions.

Since many community activities are related because of their _primary_ or _secondary_ educational purposes, they could be held or operated on the same site. In addition, these activities could be interrelated. For example, schools traditionally teach children and youth about community health practices

1

from _inside_ the classroom. If a health service was located on the school site, the health professionals could occasionally help the classroom teacher. Students might help in the clinic or visit and observe the activities of the health service.

The library-school relationship is another example of the kind of cooperative behavior that could benefit all. If the community needs a new school and a new library, both could be planned and constructed together. Using an outside entrance, the public could enter the library any time the school is opened in addition to the evening when the library is open and the rest of the school might be closed. Students could use the school/community library during the traditional daytime in addition to the evening for reference material for homework, or just for a quiet place to study.

In order to develop a clearer understanding of the above described symbiotic relationship, it is necessary to re-define "schools" and "education." We traditionally use these words as if they were synonymous; however, in this book, "schools" or "schooling" is defined as the activities of a school. "Education" is defined as the formal and informal learning activities found in the community. When using these definitions then, educational activities includes activities of schools.

Schooling and Education

Education is not something that takes place only inside a building called a school. It takes place all the time through direct experience as well as through the vicarious experiences of learning. School, therefore, must recognize as education the time young people spend outside of school, help them plan its best use, and give credit for it. Many youngsters will do better getting a larger proportion of their education outside the institution we have traditionally called school (Schiamberg, 1973).

Understanding the distinction between "schooling" and "education" is very important. It is important because it helps us discuss more clearly, the work of schools separate from other learning experiences provided by other organizations. To assume they are synonymous tends to place all learning at the doorstep of the school. Such a burden is not reasonable, given the resources available to school administrators and boards of education.

Failure to distinguish between "schooling" and "education" also allows us to ignore or discount the significant learning contributions which can be made by recreation departments, hospitals, scouting organizations, the mass media, service clubs, homeowner groups, business and industry and many other groups. Recognizing the distinction between school and education permits school officials to link with potential allies in the community to provide a healthy learning climate and specific learning opportunities for children, youth and adults at various locations throughout the community.

The Educative Community

The world about us is truly not the same as it was yesterday. Today we need new views of what can be--new approaches to meet the educational needs of our communities. Therefore, besides redefining "schooling" and "education" it would be useful to develop a new term, the "educative community." An "educative community" is one in which the inhabitants of that community value not only learning, but also assuming the role of teacher on occasion. They see themselves as occasional learners, no matter what their age.

The educative community is a place in which private and public agencies, which spend at least part of their time teaching others, see themselves as educators at heart. They are willing to share their resources with other agencies; they are willing to sit down together and cooperatively plan the implementation of programs to meet identified community needs; and they are willing to work together in order to make their own operations more efficient.

In the "educative community," the school is seen as only one force in the education process; however, it probably has a strong leadership role to play in coordinating the entire educational effort of the community. That is, it could be the responsibility of school officials in the community to raise issues related to education in order that the entire citizenry may have the opportunity to discuss and clarify what they want for their community. Issues such as equality of educational opportunity for the handicapped or minorities are rarely brought forth by school superintendents and school boards for public discussion. Sex education and the kinds of books to be

3

on required reading lists and in high school libraries could be publicly discussed. These discussions could be led by school officials at various community meetings.

Local elected officials would have similar roles to play as they help the community wrestle with other civic matters. The practical implementation of the "educative community" would involve a deliberate effort on the part of the community to identify the physical, fiscal and personnel resources available to them, determine the needs of the community, and match resources to needs. This should result in the development of programs, sponsored by civic groups and various private and public agencies of the community, which would respond to the needs of the community.

Since communities would identify schooling for the young as one of their needs, schools should play some of the traditional role of equipping youngsters with basic skills and understandings ordinarily found in the public school system. Such a community would also identify a variety of other needs. For youngsters, these might include the need for self-reliance, respect for the property of others, controlling one's temper, or developing a feeling of personal value by being invited to participate in serious problem-solving efforts of the community.

Should there be an attempt to coordinate at least some educational efforts? Each community will have to decide this for itself. There might be a financial saving if two agencies cooperate by buying land and constructing a facility big enough for both of them. Such a cooperative effort might result in better services to the community. A number of school districts in America, Canada, England and northern Europe have made the decision to jointly plan and construct educational facilities.

Rationale

Planning an educational facility can be a challenging, vital and awesome task, but it can also be an opportunity to promote community learning and development. The facility itself will exist for decades, and the myriad of learning experiences encountered there will have far-reaching effects on the community even if the facility is eventually no longer utilized as an educational center.

4

Planning is the process of making decisions in the present in order to bring about some future outcome. It involves determining appropriate goals (an educational facility) and the best means to achieve it (community involvement and support in identifying needs, expectations and wants). It becomes the "who-what-when and how" of alternative courses of action with the final or ultimate selection being that which best meets community needs.

The rationale for this planning revolves around the basic belief that a community creates the need for educational facilities, and that facility should meet the unique learning needs of the community that supports it. Ultimately, an educational facility is both a reflection of what a community is and what it hopes to become. The facility is defined by the people it serves and their developing and changing needs, interests, and aspirations.

Until recent years, <u>school</u> <u>facilities</u> were designed to facilitate the teaching of a limited population, grades K-12. A standard curriculum was taught in a standard facility, between the hours of 8:00 a.m. and 3:00 p.m. While many still espouse such ideas, some innovators believe learning can occur in a variety of facility designs, at a variety of times, and even at locations other than the "schoolhouse." There has been the advent of interest in the vocational curriculum, adult high school, pre-school day care, community enrichment, and shared community use of facilities. This, together with societal changes from an industrial to a technological to a communications-oriented society, have caused professional educators and community members to analyze and evaluate educational programs and the facilities which house them.

A community's educational needs, evolving out of societal changes and community expectations, become the functions of a given educational facility. This text accepts the premise espoused by Louis Sullivan, a renowned architect, who in 1880 is credited with suggesting that, "...form follows function," when referring to sound architectural practice (Castaldi, 1969). While in practice this dictum may not always be followed, it does seem to be reasonable advice. Educational facilities, the sites of many functions, certainly need to be planned after determining the educational functions to be housed there. While changes can be made later, to begin with no determination of educational functions would be a mistake. The chapters which follow will focus on the process of translating the many possible educational functions into the many different forms of educational facilities.

Community Education

What has been stated above is consistent with the concept of Community Education. While not all community educators would agree with the following description of Community Education, it does contain the processes found in many definitions or descriptions.

Community Education can be characterized by five processes. They are:

1. Systematically involving local citizens in the policy/decision-making process of the community's educational organizations;

2. Identifying community learning needs, and then organizing and coordinating community learning opportunities to meet these learning needs (as provided by organizations such as public and private schools, recreation departments, libraries, and others).

3. Providing formal learning opportunities for persons of all ages--the process of life-long learning;

4. Using the community's fiscal, physical, and personnel resources to enhance teaching and learning opportunities throughout the community;

5. Coordinating social agency efforts as they apply to the community's educational, or educationally-related needs.

These five processes are not programs. That is, they are means rather than ends. This is important, since the educational needs of one community are never exactly the same as those of another community. To describe Community Education as programs would suggest that each community interested in Community Education would have to adopt the same programs, even those unsuited to their current needs.

The development of educational facilities described in this text follow the Community Education processes. The planning committees for educational facilities should include local citizens and agency representatives. The determination of community needs and resources is critical at this stage of the planning process. The form of the facility should be based on a comparison of educational needs and community resources.

The Planning Process

Planning an educational facility is a comprehensive, creative process which starts with dreaming and thinking about what "might be." It then moves on to data gathering, proceeds to study and decision making, and results in the design and building of a physical plant. The chief responsibility for planning educational facilities usually rests with a government agency that has extensive experience in planning and construction. Since the facility is to be used by the community, it is vital that the planning rationale include community involvement. The community should share the planning responsibility with educationally-oriented agencies. The following "nuts and bolts" factors are characteristic of such a planning process:

1. Planning a quality educational facility will require the coordinated sharing of ideas and team decision-making efforts of a combination of many knowledgeable, interested, and concerned citizens.

2. The planning of each educational facility is a special, unique project which should meet the needs of its unique community of learners. An educational philosophy reflecting the beliefs and learning expectations of the community should be considered the foundation of the planning process.

3. A variety of data collecting, processing, studying, and interpretative activities take place in effective facility planning.

4. Facility planning is an ongoing process which does not end with the completion of the physical plant. The design should be such that changes are possible. Ongoing planning will allow for adaptation and modification of the facility to meet emerging needs of the community of learners it serves.

With these general characteristics in mind, a variety of planning processes could be designed, with various stages, steps, or descriptive flow charts, to meet the planning needs of a particular community.

Each community is different. Planning committee members are different. States have different laws regarding the construction of public facilities. This text therefore, will not suggest an inflexible or strict procedure. Instead, the planning procedure will be somewhat general in nature. As long as the above four characteristics are kept in mind, planners can use the following procedure as a general guide to encourage the prudent use of individual and agency contributions.

PHASE 1   COMMUNITY PLANNING TEAM DEVELOPMENT

PHASE 2   EDUCATIONAL PHILOSOPHY AND LEARNING THEORY CONSIDERATION

PHASE 3   DATA GATHERING

PHASE 4   DATA INTERPRETATION AND NEEDS DETERMINATION

PHASE 5   TRANSLATION OF NEEDS INTO PROGRAM PLAN DEVELOPMENT

PHASE 6   EXAMINATION OF EXISTING EDUCATIONAL PROGRAMS AND FACILITIES

PHASE 7   ENERGY USE CONSIDERATION

PHASE 8   DISCOURAGING VANDALISM

PHASE 9   TECHNOLOGY, TELECOMMUNICATIONS

PHASE 10   FACILITY PLAN FINALIZATION

PHASE 11   FACILITY PLAN IMPLEMENTATION

PHASE 12   COMMUNITY PLANNING TEAM EVALUATION

PHASE 13   DEVELOPMENT OF ONGOING EVALUATION/PLANNING PROCESS

Planning Phase Components

PHASE 1   COMMUNITY PLANNING TEAM DEVELOPMENT

Purpose: Provide for the selection of a planning team that is representative of the community to be served, will develop community ownership in the process and final product, and model characteristics of the educational facility planning process.

Process:

1. Lead agency(ies) form steering committee

2. Public meeting dates set

3. Advertisement of meetings

4. Potential members:

Business leaders	Developers
City planners	City or county
Local school personnel	commissioners
School principals	Elder citizens
Recreation department	Architect(s)
personnel	Students
Parents	School board
Political leaders	members
University educators	Social services
Religious leaders	personnel
Health services	Community service
personnel	club personnel
Ethnic/racial	Construction
representatives	personnel
Youth groups (Boy and	Professional
Girl Scouts, etc.)	consultant(s)

5. Community members volunteer, others recruited by steering committee

6. Decision by new planning team members as to any additional members who might be needed to form a community committee with sufficient representation

7. Group formally organized--steering committee dissolved

8. Meeting dates set

9. Meeting format determined

10. Information disseminated to the public

PHASE 2   EDUCATIONAL PHILOSOPHY AND   LEARNING   THEORY
CONSIDERATIONS

Purpose: With the possible assistance of others,
planning team discusses various philosophies of
education. Understanding educational philosophy, even
at an elementary level, will assist the planners to
develop a statement of mission or goal for their work.
Such a discussion, when coupled with a discussion of
learning theory, will help the planners to more fully
realize why "form" should be determined after
determining "function."

Process:

1.   Examine philosophies of education:
                          Perennialism
                          Essentialism
                          Progressivism
                          Existentialism

2.   Examine learning theory of:
                          Children
                          Youth
                          Adults
                          Elder Americans

3.   Determine implications of learning theory
      and philosophy of education on construction

PHASE 3   DATA GATHERING

Purpose: Determine current needs and wants of
community members in order to make community-relevant
program and facility decisions.

Process:

1.   Sensing general community interests

2.   Locating potential community partners

3.   Collection of data, existing and new

PHASE 4   DATA INTERPRETATION AND NEEDS DETERMINATION

Purpose: Raw data is not sufficient. The data must be
interpreted and eventually restated in terms of
community needs and wants.

Process:

    1. Count, collate, analyze, etc.
       a. Entire team
       b. Study groups as needed

    2. Develop list of needs, wants

    3. Disseminate information to public

PHASE 5   NEEDS TRANSLATED INTO PROGRAM PLAN DEVELOPMENT

Purpose: Develop programs to meet these needs and wants.

Process:

    1. Rank order needs
       a. Entire team
       b. Study groups as needed

    2. Develop program plan to meet priority needs
       a. Entire group
       b. Study groups as needed

    3. Disseminate information to the public

    4. Planning team members share results of effort with specific groups they represent

PHASE 6   EXAMINE EXISTING EDUCATIONAL PROGRAMS AND FACILITIES AND SELECT SITE, IF NEEDED, FOR NEW FACILITY

Purpose: Eliminate unnecessary duplication. Examine the possibility of housing new programs in existing facilities.

Process:

    1. Examine existing facilities for unused space

    2. Study current government and agency policies regarding possible cooperative behavior

    3. Study financial requirements of proposed new programs

4. Determine best location for site of new
    facility in relationship to needs, and in
    consideration of the location of existing
    educational facilities

PHASE 7   ENERGY USE CONSIDERATIONS

Purpose: Develop the most energy-efficient facility
possible.

Process:

1. Study possible building orientation to
    sun's path and prevailing winds

2. Maintain existent vegetation which has
    potential for energy conservation

3. Consider building designs which have pass-
    ive energy conservation potential, such as
    window space and location, roof overhang,
    etc.

4. Disseminate information to the public

PHASE 8   DISCOURAGING VANDALISM

Purpose: Develop social and physical plant design that
will tend to mitigate against vandalism.

Process:

1. Define various damage-producing behaviors

2. Develop plan for instituting social van-
    dalism-prevention considerations

3. Develop floor plan considerations that will
    tend to preclude vandalism

4. Disseminate information to the public

PHASE 9   TECHNOLOGY, TELECOMMUNICATIONS

Purpose: Provide users of facility with "smart"
building--one ready to facilitate use of latest
technology for energy conservation, communications,
discouraging of vandalism, manipulation of data.

Process:

1. Plan for hardware, people and environmental needs

2. Consider technical requirements for the use of various size computers

3. Determine management/supervision training needs if computer training or large computers to be located in facility

4. Disseminate information to public

PHASE 10   FACILITY FLOOR PLAN FINALIZATION

Purpose: Develop general floor and site plans based upon all data and information now available.

Process:

1. Review data from studies

2. Develop facility plan

3. Disseminate information to the public

4. Planning team members share results of effort with specific groups they represent

PHASE 11   FACILITY PLAN IMPLEMENTATION

Purpose: Implement agency-required process for construction or renovation of facility.

Process:

1. Implementation of construction process by appropriate agency

2. Planning team meets regularly to review facility plan implementation progress

3. Disseminate information to the public

PHASE 12   COMMUNITY PLANNING TEAM EVALUATION

Purpose: Evaluation of planning process to learn from this planning experience.

13

Process:

Determine if the educational facility "form" is serving the "functions" as determined in PHASE 5.

PHASE 13 DEVELOPMENT OF ONGOING EVALUATION/PLANNING PROCESS

Purpose: Develop procedure for continuous monitoring of facility use in relation to changing community needs.

Process:

1. Determine who will be responsible for ongoing facility evaluation
   a. Entire team?
   b. Study groups?
   c. New or expanded team?

2. Determine when the evaluation/planning team will meet

3. Disseminate information to the public

REFERENCE

Schiamberg, Lawrence B. (1973). <u>Adolescent alienation</u>, Columbus, Ohio: Charles E. Merrill Publishing Co., p. 123.

Castaldi, Basil (1969). <u>Educational facilities</u>, Chicago: Rand McNally & Company, p. 13.

CHAPTER 2

BEGINNING WITH FUNCTION RATHER THAN FORM

Many people know how to build a public school. Using a combination of local and state funds, land is purchased, an architect is hired to draw the plans and a general contractor is engaged to build the desired facility. Those steps plus a hundred others will result in a school building.

Unfortunately, although many people think they know how to build a school, they may get halfway through the project before they discover that something was left out of the plans, or that at this late date, a better procedure could have been used to accomplish the task. If people ask the right questions before they get too far into a building project, they can avoid unnecessary frustration, expense and wasted time.

The purpose of this chapter is to remind the reader of questions that are often not asked when designing and constructing educational facilities. These questions deal with educational philosophy and learning theory, which are topics many people avoid.

Discussing philosophy need not be a painful experience. Philosophies of life are not difficult to understand nor boring to discuss. The entire matter can be enjoyable.

For a facility to have the greatest chance for meeting community needs, questions about philosophy and learning must be asked and answered. The answers can then be used in almost all other steps of the planning process. While no building design will prevent or guarantee certain teaching or learning strategies, the building design can certainly encourage or hinder such strategies.

Consider teaching and learning styles. Teaching styles are based upon one's educational philosophy and personality. Teaching style or preference can vary from teaching large groups to providing individualized learning experiences, from minimal use of technology as

15

a teaching aid to the use of sophisticated technology for the purpose of complete individualization of learning. The large group/minimal technology style requires rooms large enough to accommodate groups of thirty to one-hundred or more, and a few basic, technology devices (such as film projector and screen, or a TV monitor and video tape playback machine) and the required electrical outlets.

For small group or individualized teaching and maximum use of technology, rooms will be required that can accommodate individual learning carrels, special wiring (conduits and raceways to hold the wiring which are large enough to add new wiring), and a flexible room plan to allow easy movement from individual learning to small-group learning.

As for learning styles, most young learners, (and some older ones) benefit most from considering concrete examples of the world around them, and having the opportunity to closely examine the actual thing. Older learners can usually learn from abstract ideas. The "concrete" learners can benefit from laboratories-- places to observe the natural change in animals, plants, or minerals, and where they have opportunities for hands-on experiences. This style will require a different facility than that for those learners who learn from handling and manipulating abstract ideas.

Encouraging an exploration of educational philosophy and learning theory is not meant to lead the reader into thinking exclusively about schools. Any facility intended for the purpose of meeting educational needs such as libraries, hospitals, businesses or government agencies, should be designed with a consideration of educational philosophy and learning theory. The point is not that only one or two specific philosophies/theories should be accommodated; rather, a building should be designed to accommodate a variety of teaching and learning styles based upon an educational philosophy/theory.

At the planning stage, no one may know which teachers, learners or group facilitators will eventually work in this facility. Therefore, planners should be aware of all the possibilities and plan appropriate building flexibility.

A brief discussion of educational philosophy and learning theory at the beginning of the planning process might prevent an embarrassing situation later when someone asks why the design does or does not facilitate certain teaching/learning opportunities. To say the planners neglected to address that issue would be unfortunate.

Philosophies of Education

Philosophies or theories of education come from philosophies of life. The following pages will briefly describe these philosophies/theories of education.

Since the following descriptions are necessarily only an introduction to these philosophies, the reader is encouraged to read other texts. The descriptions are not presented in any special order. Each is derived from other philosophies about life in general and each makes its own contribution to our further understanding of the special world of education. (See Figure 1)

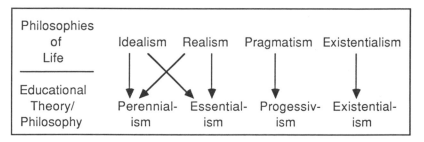

Figure 1. The philosophy of life continuum in relationship to educational theory/philosophy.

While history records several philosophies of life, the reader should not be restricted in the interpretations of these philosophies by mentally compartmentalizing them as separate and distinct units. Lines that are drawn and separate explanations that are made are done to assist the reader in coming to a basic understanding of each.

When considering philosophies of life as possible sources of inspiration toward the development of a learning organization, their relatedness, similarities and differences should allow us to perceive them as forming a continuum from Idealism to Realism to Pragmatism to Existentialism. The educational theories or philosophies follow the same continuum since they are derived from these philosophies of life.

Current public school teaching generally falls into the Essentialism and Progressivism areas. Perennialism, with its reliance on the Great Books series and church dogma, is seldom found in public school organizations today. The same can be said for Existentialism. Existentialism is relatively new, and its emphasis on individual judgment would make it difficult to implement in public schools where emphasis is also placed on group conformity. Therefore, while a brief explanation is provided of these two educational theories/philosophies, no comment will be offered regarding their implications for educational facility design.

Essentialism

By its very name, essentialism gives us a clue to its meaning for educators. Supporters of essentialism believe there are essential facts and ideas that all learners must master. The important facts and ideas generally come from the study of science, mathematics, literature, and history.

Here the learner is viewed as having a mind like a blank tablet which needs to be filled with information in order to help him/her grow mentally into a person able to function effectively in our society.

With essentialism, the learner can also be viewed as a sense mechanism. We enter the world with five senses which make possible our learning about the world of facts and ideas.

The role of the teacher (or librarian, recreation director, trainer, etc.) is to demonstrate the essential facts and ideas and to be an example of an individual who has acquired the needed information for successful living. Not only can the teacher tell the learner some of this essential information, but it can be shared with learners through textbooks, films or other secondary sources.

Essentialism promotes the idea that the prime function of the school is to preserve and transmit the basic elements of human culture. Schools must not be allowed to degenerate into mindless institutions that cater to transitory facts or to childish whims.

Life's experiences suggest the apparent truth of essentialism. Newborn learners seem to have very little information tucked away in their heads. They

18

also have sense mechanisms in order to know what is happening around them. We want these new learners to become successful adults who know about the ideas and information of the world. These adults carefully use their senses to determine when and how to use the knowledge they have, in order to be successful.

Perennialism

Perennialists see intellectual and spiritual mastery and development as the crucial factors in education. Learners are more than mere sense mechanisms or empty-headed people. Learners are thinking people. They daily wrestle with ideas. Sometimes people jump to conclusions while at other times they carefully think through problems or situations and arrive at conclusions. But only those with the self-discipline to discard their own biases and short-sightedness have a chance to find truth.

Learners are spiritual beings. They live on earth in relation to a higher being. They need to examine this relationship in order that their acts, as a result of disciplined thinking, are also tempered with their understanding of right and wrong. Perennialists believe that with a trained intellect and communion with God, a more enlightened human behavior is possible.

The word "perennialism" also suggests the basic point about this educational philosophy--that the human condition is unchanging. The problems we face today-- greed, lust, poverty, discrimination, gluttony and others--are the same ones faced by people living hundreds of years ago. The problems are perennial, recurring over and over. One has only to view some of today's television soap operas and Hollywood movies, and compare their themes with the Seven Deadly Sins from the Middle Ages, to confirm the perennial nature of human problems.

Since the problems are perennial, learners can look to writings from the past for help in knowing how to deal with these problems today. Textbooks for the perennialist teacher would include the Great Books series and books of religious dogma. Writings in these books have already described and discussed the basic problems of humanity and the relationship of humans to a higher Being. Mathematics and the study of logic must also be part of the training of the intellect.

Progressivism

As early as the 1890's, and all the way up through the 1930's and early 40's, some educational philosophers were beginning to see in young learners a different truth about learning. While not rejecting statements from the essentialists and perennialists, they did state a different essence about the learner and learning. The learner is not simply a blank slate or sense mechanism, nor just a rational and spiritual being. Rather, the learner is someone who _experiences_ the world daily. As learners, we sense the world around us, we think about it, and we learn new ideas. More importantly, we connect our current experiences with past knowledge and experiences into a total, interrelated understanding of the present moment.

Learning unrelated facts is nonsense. For things to be learned and to experience the joy of learning one must be able to relate the learning to the learner's world. To do this will require a teacher who has the primary role of guide and advisor rather than dispenser of facts. The teaching methodology is one of problem-solving.

For example, an individual learner, or a group of learners might want to assist younger students in learning more about the history of their city. With the teacher as facilitator, mentor, mature adult and guide, the learners might eventually produce their own local history book. In this way the learners have not only experienced the joy of having made a significant contribution to society but, in the process, learned spelling, grammar, writing, interviewing, problem-solving, book-printing, art, history and acquired other knowledge/skills. In this experience, learning has become exciting and related to the real world.

Existentialism

During the 1930's and 40's, the world learned about a new philosophy called existentialism. As with the other philosophies of life, this too has a statement to make about education. In this philosophy the essence of learning is discovering how to make responsible, ethical choices. During our waking hours we are constantly making choices--to read or daydream, to follow the rules or challenge them, to answer another's call for help or ignore it, to prepare for the examination or not. Daily living is filled with making choices. Young learners need opportunities to discuss life's choices and the consequences of these choices with the classroom teacher.

Teachers who use existentialism as their teaching strategy know a lot about themselves. They understand how to make choices and they provoke learners to try to think more clearly about the process of choosing. With a teacher's assistance, learners will learn why others in history made the choices they did and what were the consequences of those choices.

Implications for Building Design

No building design can or should force the abandonment of a particular educational philosophy. Hopefully, the building design will facilitate any teaching/learning style used by any teacher-learner-facilitator working in this facility.

Essentialism stresses the training of the intellect through the five senses. Teachers who believe in essentialism see learners as blank tablets. If learners are provided with information through their five senses, then these learners will be able to enjoy the world about them. Therefore, the physical setting needed would include large halls where many learners at once can be give information through lectures, viewing films or seeing plays. Space would also be needed for quiet reading, and for some small group areas for learners who need extra help. Walls would probably be of neutral colors in order not to distract learners from their basic task of acquiring information.

The building should be operational year around. There is no need for children to vacate the building during the summer. The sooner the learners get the information they need, the better off they will be.

Progressive advocates would probably wish for a multi-purpose, colorful and exciting building. It could be made exciting by the presence of modern science laboratories, computers, television sets and interesting display areas; by easy access to the outdoors and availability of plots of ground or windowsills for growing things; and by providing workshop areas. Traditional classrooms would also be needed because learners would occasionally be gathered for large group lessons, for viewing films, or for other large group meetings. Smaller areas would also be required as these learners are encouraged to form groups to work on classroom or community projects.

The building should also be designed as an especially safe place no matter what the educational philosophy. It must be noticeably secure against those who would try to enter the building for evil purposes, from hazards, storms, or any other act that would disturb learning. The learners must not spend time worrying about their safety--they need to spend their time learning.

Learning/Teaching Strategies

The goals of learning, and personal teaching/learning styles determine learning and teaching strategies. Generally, the goals of learning are to have learners master certain fundamental facts/ideas and help them develop self-confidence in their own ability to learn. Acquiring information is certainly a goal of learning--people believe that acquiring such information is necessary to satisfy their present or future requirements. At the same time, the process of acquiring these ideas or basic facts should enable us to experience the joy of learning and help us attain faith in our own ability to solve our problems.

The achievement of these goals has historically been promoted by two theories of learning. One is called associationism (stimulus-response, behaviorism, guided, structured, traditional); the other is called cognitive-field theory (Gestalt, free, open, progressive). Associationism is linked with Pavlov, Watson, Thorndike and Skinner. Cognitive-field theory is associated with Bruner, Dewey, Kohl, Kozol and Dennison. (See Figure 2)

Associationism can be characterized as a teacher-centered approach to helping learners obtain facts and ideas in the most efficient and effective manner possible. Students are guided in their learning by being given structured learning experiences. Based upon the concept of stimulus-response, teachers will tell, or otherwise provide, learners certain facts and ideas (stimulus) in the belief that in the telling, (content and process) teachers can provoke the retention of these facts and ideas.

Getting someone to respond with the correct answer can be approached in two ways within associationism. One is to obtain elicited behavior which is a pre-determined physiological or psychological response when presented the same stimulus each time. This is an

22

unsatisfactory teaching method since we would want learners to take care of their needs under a variety of situations. Therefore the followers of associationism prefer obtaining emitted behavior which is a teaching style that encourages learning through a variety of conditions. An example of this might be in teaching addition where the teacher attempts to increase learning by showing the learner the flash card with 2 + 2 = ? on it. The teacher would also want the learner to be able to add when given two pennies to add to two other pennies or any sets of two groups each.

<u>Learning Goals</u>
Mastery of fundamental ideas
Self-confidence in one's ability to learn

<u>Associationism</u>   <u>Cognitive-field</u> <u>Theory</u>
(Stimulus-response, behaviorism) (Gestalt, free, open,)
(guided, structured, traditional)   (progressive)

(Pavlov, Watson, Thorndike,)   (Bruner, Dewey, Kohl,)
       (Skinner)   (Kozol, Dennison)

<u>Figure</u> 2.   Two paths to learning goals

     Proof of retention is found in responses found on test papers and obtained through classroom recitation. Material retained can be used by learners to satisfy their daily needs and, at the same time, to obtain increased confidence in their future ability to provide for their needs and wants.

     The traditional classroom in America is one in which teachers plan out each lesson and each day. The learners are required to obtain facts and ideas from books, workbooks, films and/or teacher lectures, and repeat back to the teacher what each learner remembers. This is similar to the associationism approach to achieving the goals of learning.

     Cognitive-field theory suggests a learner-centered approach whereby the learner is invited to help choose topics or problems for study. The learner may discover facts and ideas in a sequence that may differ from the sequence desired by other learners or from the sequence by which the teacher learned the same or similar ideas.

Those supportive of the cognitive-field theory of learning believe that we learn not only by receiving stimuli through our senses, but also by taking these outside stimuli and combining them with ideas already in our heads. In this way we can come to conclusions not already learned in past experiences. In other words, we exercise our ability of insight.

The teacher's primary role is one of developing a classroom atmosphere or learning environment that invites and encourages learners to initiate their own attempt to obtain facts and ideas needed to solve problems important to the learner, the teacher, or both. This encouragement is done by providing learners with a carefully structured series of questions that invite insightful, spontaneous conclusions. Once learners acquire the problem-solving approach to issues, they may wish to choose their own topic of interest to pursue as an individual project. In this way, the teacher makes use of the learner's own drive to explore the world, to solve personally important problems. This teaching strategy releases learners to become all they are capable of becoming.

Both of these theories have implications for the design of a learning center. The associationism theory that stresses the efficiency and effectiveness of learning directed by a teacher would suggest classrooms similar to what we observe in most American schools today. Most of the classrooms can be described as having a teacher-pupil ratio of one to twenty-five or thirty, with all seats facing the teacher's desk at the front of the classroom. The chalkboards are located on the front and side walls, and most class activities are directed and controlled by the teacher from the front of the room.

The cognitive-field theory of learning needs a facility that allows the learner to perform many different activities. A building design that would facilitate this theory would provide for large and small group activity areas as well as areas for individual study. Sufficient storage areas for reference materials would be available as well as locations for experimenting with plants and physical objects. Easy access to other areas of the building and the outside grounds would be important; a small theater and/or performing arts area would also be helpful. Learners would need access to computers and

24

information stored on laser discs and in mainframe computers at other locations. This access to data in other locations will require telephone lines connected to at least some of the classroom computers. A satellite dish on the facility grounds would also be needed in order to receive information from other sources.

Characteristics of Various Learners

In addition to philosophies of education and learning theory, the facility planning committee should become familiar with the physical and mental characteristics of various age learners. If the community to be served by this facility is composed of learners of various ages, these characteristics will have implications for the design of the facility.

Some of the many characteristics of learners which should be taken into account when designing the facility are described in the following paragraphs.

Preschool and Kindergarten, ages 3-6

These children like to run, jump, skip and climb. Give them plenty of room and opportunities to safely exercise their large leg and arm muscles.

Large muscle activities soon require the learner to rest. The area for this age learner needs to be designed so that it can become a quiet rest area.

Children of this age do not yet have the ability to see fine print. Therefore, letters of the alphabet and numbers will have to be larger than those found in classrooms or activity areas for older learners.

Children of this age group tend to easily form different play/learning groups. Therefore, as much space as possible will be needed by this age group as they move from one group to another.

Preschoolers like to play at being different people--mothers, dads, police officer, and others. Try to plan a stage area for this group. Children of this age are highly inventive and imaginative. This characteristic can be handled by providing opportunities for using clay, paint and other "expressive" materials. Storage areas will be needed as well as appropriate floor covering.

Primary Grades, ages 6-9

These, too, are very active children. They will need places for the exercise of large muscles. As with the 3-6 age group, this one too, will need opportunities for rest.

Most children's eyes are not fully developed until about age eight, therefore, these children's materials should include large print and numbers. Children in this age group can enjoy some small group games. Provision for such play areas should be taken into account by the planning committee.

Language ability is quite good in this age span. Places for plays, readings, creative poems and other presentations would be appreciated by this group of learners.

Upper Elementary, ages 9-12

Small muscle ability is much improved by this age. Areas for music, arts and crafts, drawing and other activities requiring the use of small muscles can be incorporated in the building design.

Since large muscle growth is continuing, Playgrounds and gyms will also be important areas for this age group.

Curiosity abounds in this age span. Since exploratory activities are needed here, storage cabinets and supervised experimental work areas will be needed.

Junior High, ages 12-15

At this age span, the physical and mental development is the most widespread of any age group. Therefore, opportunities for a wide range of activities should be provided. Such activities might include small group or individual study, whole group activities, music and art presentations, large group games, stage or theater productions, and individual or small group discovery/learning centers.

Learners in this age group may occasionally daydream, can comprehend abstract concepts to an increasing degree, are more objective about the infallibility of adults, and can be intolerant and opinionated. Opportunities to discuss moral and political issues in debates and plays could be a constructive way to allow junior high students to express their needs. Areas for plays and debates would help meet the needs of this group of learners.

Senior High, ages 15-18

As with the junior high age group, this group also has tremendous physical and mental differences. Therefore, a variety of opportunities and physical activity areas will be needed in order to serve this group well.

The move from childhood to adulthood takes place during this age span. Areas for shops, music, drama and all the other opportunities to experiment and achieve a degree of competency in adult-like activities is important. Learners in this age group can work more independently than at an earlier age. Areas that provide for independence such as individual study carrels, music practice rooms, and access to computers are important.

The Adult Learner

Adult learners are obviously different than those previously discussed. They are usually part-time rather than full-time learners when involved in formal learning, and are voluntary, rather than compulsory students. Most adults are capable of assisting in the planning, execution, and evaluation of their own learning activities.

Educational programs for adults should include provisions for self-directed learning and for self-evaluation. The facility can support this type of learning program by providing for computer-assisted instruction, video-taping, individual and small group study areas and easy access to reference materials.

Provisions might also be made to deal with any decrease in visual and/or auditory acuity which may occur with aging as well as other physical impairments. Additionally, educational facility planners for this group should consider the transportation methods used by adult learners since school buses are not usually available for the adult learner. Where parking lots are provided, they should be of adequate size and well-lighted since many adult classes are held during evening hours.

Learning and the Older Adult

While the older adult will probably learn (psychologically) in the same manner as anyone else, many have undergone some important physical changes. These changes should be considered by the design team if the population to be served includes elder Americans.

The visual acuity of many of our elder Americans is reduced. Adaptation to darkness is slowed, vision is narrowed, and many need glasses. Therefore, provisions should be made for larger print, sufficient and even amounts of light from the parking lot to the classroom, and well-marked steps or ramps.

There is a greater amount of hearing loss among elder Americans than the general population. If such a loss is not corrected, suspiciousness, feelings of inadequacy, frustration and anxiety can be the result. Therefore, the designers need to be concerned about the elimination of background noises such as air conditioning, or noises from other classrooms. Provision might even be made for microphones and loudspeakers in some classrooms or large meeting rooms used by the older citizens.

CHAPTER 3

MEETING COMMUNITY NEEDS

The process of planning and developing an educational facility has two major goals. One is to construct an educational facility that meets the needs of the community. The second is to encourage full citizen involvement in activities of the facility when it is completed. Only when the process is well thought-out and implemented can both of these goals be achieved.

Planning and implementation processes that involve only a few people may result in producing a facility that meets the needs of those few people. Widespread involvement of citizens has the potential of helping the planning committee discover many more community needs. It also has the potential of convincing citizens that the facility is not for a select group since everyone was invited to participate in the planning process. By inviting community involvement at the beginning, credibility can be built between the planners of the new facility and the people the facility was designed to serve. While it is possible to attain credibility after opening the doors of the facility, why not get a head start by involving people from the beginning of the planning process?

Getting Started

The planning committee should consider establishing a sub-committee on citizen needs to be chaired by a member of the planning committee. "Community needs" is a term used by the author to encompass both wants and needs. "Needs" includes such basic requirements as food, shelter, health care and companionship. "Wants" may include features such as having access to computers or stock market information and attending social and cultural functions--items which would certainly be considered desirable by many people but would not be necessities for all. Local citizens could be appointed as members of this sub-committee which would report to the planning committee through the sub-committee chairperson. In this way, the planning committee is not enlarged beyond a manageable size but more citizens would be involved in the planning process.

To succeed, the chairperson of this sub-committee will need the appropriate skills to provide leadership, conduct meetings, and generally to direct and monitor the work of the sub-committee.

Before beginning the process of determining community needs, the sub-committee should develop a plan for achieving its goal. The following suggestions are offered as an effective and efficient plan to determine community needs:

1.   Orienting sub-committee to the task

2.   Sensing general community interests

3.   Locating potential community partners

4.   Determining specific plan

5.   Collecting existing data

6.   Collecting new data

7.   Translating data into community needs

8.   Translating needs into potential programs

9.   Determining existing community facilities

10. Establishing general building requirements

11. Exploring financial resources

Step One: Orientation

The sub-committee on community needs, which will make recommendations to the planning committee, should be oriented to the entire educational facility planning process so they can appreciate how their work will coordinate with the work of others. They also need to understand the parameters of their work and resources available which might include the following: geographical area of community to be surveyed; amount of money available (if any) for postage, printing, consultants, etc.; date sub-committee report is due; assistance available from community organizations that are interested in this educational facility, such as public schools, city recreation department or others; and any other restrictions or resources impacting on their work.

After the sub-committee has received a general orientation to the task, a specific plan of how the group will work together needs to be developed. Such a plan should include determining how the group will make decisions within its own operation, how assignments will be given to each member of the group, how the group wishes to handle internal conflict, and other group process details.

Step Two: Sensing General Interests

The sub-committee might begin by holding a few community meetings to determine, in a general way, what the citizens would like to see in their new facility. Holding the meetings in a variety of places would encourage widespread participation by many segments of the population. Information obtained as a result of these meetings can be used when the balance of the sub-committee's plan for achieving their goal is outlined.

There are two main advantages to this step of the process. First, it provides an opportunity for the sub-committee to get a general sense of the community's interests. Without this information, the sub-committee might make plans without considering community needs that should have been addressed in earlier committee work. To go back and collect the data at this point would be an unfortunate loss of the committee's time and energy.

Second, this step provides for the initial involvement of additional community members. Such involvement will help to build trust between the sub-committee and the community, thereby increasing the possibility for community cooperation in the collection of community data.

Step Three: Looking for Partners

The sub-committee should inform local social service agencies and government offices about the upcoming survey of community needs. In this way, any of these agencies or offices planning a survey of their own, can explore the possibility of conducting a survey in cooperation with the sub-committee. Such a cooperative effort could save time, money, and personal effort for all groups.

Step Four: A Specific Plan

Once the community's needs have been determined and cooperative efforts with others explored, a step-by-step plan needs to be adopted so the group can achieve its goal by the target date. Such a plan should place the required steps in proper sequence; assign responsibility for each step; determine resources (money, materials, people) needed for each step; decide how each step will be completed; and establish a completion date for each step. This complete plan shall then be published and distributed to all members of the sub-committee and to the mass media. The plan can also be shared with the members of the educational facility planning group for approval or information, depending upon the approved procedure.

Step Five: Existing Data

After the sub-committee decides on a plan of "who will do what and when," the actual data collection concerning community needs is ready to begin. Existing data can be gathered from a variety of community sources. The sub-committee would be wise to identify and utilize this data to avoid costly and time-consuming duplication of efforts.

Following are suggested sources for existing data.

1.   Local, county and state government offices usually have information about the community. Police, fire, planning and building departments also have information about the community from which needs could be inferred. In addition, county or state health or employment offices and offices of social services can provide the committee with information about the community to be served by the facility.

2.   U. S. Census. In slow-changing communities, this data is frequently useful even seven or eight years after it was collected. The data is presented in tables by census tract, county or parish areas, and by state. Most libraries have a copy for their state. Knowing the unemployment rate, number of citizens at various income categories, number of citizens at

various age levels and other such demographic data makes possible inferences about citizen needs.

3. Large businesses. Many large businesses gather information about their customers or potential customers. Depending on the kind of information available, it could be useful to the sub-committee.

Step Six: New Data

Once existing data has been collected, the sub-committee might need more information, based on what was discovered during Step Two (Sensing General Interests). Additional information may also help clarify the needs discovered by analyzing the existing data. The following people and organizations are additional sources of information about the community.

1. Volunteer or civic organizations. These organizations usually have information about the community as a result of their close contact with local citizens. Examples of such organizations are the Red Cross, Lions Club, Rotary, Kiwanis, Girl and Boy Scouts, 4-H Club, and the Urban League.

2. Key people. By the nature of their work or interests, some individuals in the community have the opportunity to take part in certain community activities and are, therefore, especially well informed about the community as a whole, or about certain aspects of it. Such people may be government officials (elected officials or administrators of various departments), business owners, social or neighborhood leaders.

3. Local citizenry. The people to be served can advise the subcommittee about their own interests. The very process of surveying citizens by written questionnaire, telephone or community meetings, invites them to be a significant part of this process, and lets them know their ideas are important--that they can influence the decision-making process.

4. People with special roles in the community can provide first-hand information about local needs. People in this category include family-

service counselors, religious leaders, social workers, visiting nurses, physicians, state employment service interviewers, labor union business agents, educators, recreation directors, librarians and hospital directors of training.

5. Mass media representatives have information about community needs. People in this category include newspaper editors and reporters, producers of local television programs, and radio talk-show personalities. These individuals are trained to be sensitive to pressure points in the personal lives of the population they serve. Such sensitivity provides clues about trends in the changing patterns of individual needs.

6. Professional literature such as journals in the fields of education, psychology, sociology, anthropology, political science, religion, economics, business, science, humanities and social work carry articles which may yield insight into the needs of people.

Step Seven: Translating Data Into Needs

The translation of data into needs is a process that should involve not only the sub-committee members but others as well. Having others involved minimizes the possibility of committee member bias. Since the committee members have been observing this data for several weeks as they collected it, some may have already come to conclusions before all the data has been collected. Others not on this committee might bring a different perspective or viewpoint that will allow the data to be seen a little differently. Such diversity should be seen as helpful to the task; it will provide a more accurate reading of community needs.

The collected data will need to be sorted into various groups or categories and analyzed one category at a time. The data to be presented should be visually displayed with wall charts or in booklets since the group will need to refer to the data several times before coming to any conclusions.

Once all the data has been presented and translated into needs, the entire list of needs should be reviewed. This should be done to discover

34

significant relationships that might exist between needs.

Step Eight: Translating Needs Into Programs

Individual and grouped needs can now be translated into specific programs by asking the question, "What program(s) are required to meet this community need?". Asking for help from experts and organizations who currently have some responsibility in these program areas is necessary for the successful determination of programs.

During the discussion of matching programs to needs, sub-committee members have another important role--that of offering a friendly challenge to the experts concerning their suggestions of the kinds of programs to be designed to meet the expressed needs.

Experts and agency representatives are not immune to their own biases; citizens may challenge their thinking and recommendations in order to produce the best thinking of all involved.

Step Nine: Determining Existing Facilities

Once a determination has been made about the need for new programs, the sub-committee should not necessarily conclude that all programs should be housed in the new facility. A government, or private or non-profit agency might accept responsibility for implementing one or more of the programs. Since previous steps in this suggested process recommended inclusion of government and agency directors, their past involvement should help to pave the way for a discussion of the possibility of agencies taking on new programs or expanding some of their current offerings to meet newly discovered needs. To ignore existing facilities controlled by other organizations is a violation of the concept of planning and implementing Community Education facilities.

Step Ten: Establishing Building Requirements

After the list of recommended programs for the new Community Education facility has been generated, the sub-committee should invite a new group of knowledgeable individuals to discuss the details of these building needs. These individuals should be people in the community currently working as program administrators or government/agency staff members with expertise in these program areas. They would be a good source for obtaining detailed recommendations about the kind of rooms, storage areas and other specific facilities needed for the successful implementation of the programs. This new group will likely become supporters of the project by virtue of their involvement.

Step Eleven: Financial Resources

There are a variety of funding sources for educational facility construction dollars. The planning committee will want to give each its full consideration.

> 1. City and/or county government facilities that will serve city and/or county citizens can justifiably be constructed partly with city and county funds. The use of the facility in delivering services to community clients (city and/or county) by a variety of agencies is a relatively small expense compared to costs of construction and operation when each agency has its own facility.

> 2. State funds. State governments traditionally help local school districts by providing some school construction funds. For example, the State of Florida specifically provides funding for the construction of community educational facilities as described in this document under provisions of Florida Statutes Section 235.196.

> 3. Federal funds. While the availability of these funds is determined yearly, the potential is always present. A letter to the U. S. Department of Education, or to one's senator or representative can obtain the latest information about these funds.

> 4. Private foundations. Many libraries contain books that describe hundreds of local, state and national foundations. Some will provide construction funds for approved projects. Carefully written letters that discuss the multi-use educational facility could be sent to all such foundations for the purpose of exploring possible construction grants.

The sub-committee is now ready to make its recommendations to the planning committee in a written report. In addition to a description of the proposed physical facility, the report should provide appropriate background information. This information should describe the relationship of the final construction requirements to programs that respond to community needs--programs that were identified from data elicited from the community.

CHAPTER 4

ENERGY USE CONSIDERATIONS

The energy crisis of 1973, a record cold winter of 1977, the extreme summer heat in much of the United States, and the cost of oil and gas have made energy conservation a must for planners, builders and managers of educational facilities.

Marian Wilson furnishes the following statistic for planners to consider as they design educational facilities: "Buildings consume about one-third of all the energy used in this country. The U. S. National Bureau of Standards has conducted studies which indicate about forty percent of that energy is wasted. Much of this is attributed to the design and lavish use of glass" (Wilson, 1981). Other energy-related facts come from the Educational Facilities Laboratories and from Shirley Neill. "The average American uses about nine times as much energy as the average (person in other parts of the world)" (Educational Facilities Laboratories, 1973). "The United States, with six percent of the world's population, consumes about one-third of its energy" (Neill, 1977).

These statistics should help planners focus on two key points about energy:

1. Energy-conserving facility <u>design</u> is necessary to cut the high use of energy by educational facilities

2. Ongoing energy conservation by the facility manager is essential after completion of the energy-efficient facility

Energy-Efficient Facility Design

Designing a new educational facility provides the opportunity to take a conservation approach to energy use from "day one." Since energy efficiency in buildings is partially tied directly to construction, planning for efficient energy use before the first

brick is laid is obviously of vital importance.
Fortunately, much more is known about energy
conservation today than in past decades. Research and
technological development have provided us with
information which can be helpful in designing energy-
efficient facilities. The cost of energy should serve
as a stimulus to greater use of this energy
information.

The educational facility planning committee should
consider developing energy goals prior to developing
the building design. Such goals have the potential of
constantly reminding the committee of the seriousness
of energy conservation. For example, the committee
might decide that energy consumption for the new
facility will have to be less than for current
buildings of similar size and function. The same type
of goal could be set for remodeled buildings. The
redesigned facility should use less energy than the
original structure. The fact that the community will
pay the energy bills in future years is an added
incentive for the planning committee.

The committee is invited to consider some of the
following suggestions and ideas as they develop the
energy-efficient educational facility:

1.   Seek Professional Assistance

Formulating energy plans for a facility is a
difficult task and the help of a professional
trained in energy conservation would be helpful
to the committee. It would also be helpful to
have an architect/engineer with an interest in
energy conservation.

Other sources of assistance to the committee
might be sought from local utility companies,
state/federal agencies, or local universities.

2.   Life-Cycle Costing

Planners will need to evaluate a variety of
systems in terms of initial and long-range
energy conservation costs. Facility planners
may want to consider selecting initially higher
cost systems if they yield a lower long-range
cost due to long-term energy savings.

3.   Facility Size

The size of the educational facility should be

determined by the functions it will serve. The goal of meeting community needs and desires may result in a multi-purpose facility used beyond the usual working day.

While some say a multi-purpose facility must be larger and, therefore, use more energy, this may not be the case. Some energy specialists suggest we look at the community as a whole, as a total system of energy users. The people using the educational facility would be at other service facilities or in their own homes if needed services were not provided at the educational site. The resulting use of energy at home by individuals might be greater than that expended at the educational facility when residents are there as a group. Studies have shown that a multi-use facility can actually save energy when the community is viewed as a whole.

It is important to keep the building size as small as possible and still meet the size requirements of the functions it will serve. Planners must avoid wasted space and the resultant waste in energy.

4. Building Shape

The shape of a facility can affect the energy consumption level of the facility. The more wall and roof surface areas, the more potential for heat loss and gain. Outside walls are energy expensive. A rambling, one-story facility composed of several connected buildings will probably be the highest energy user, all other factors remaining the same. A one-story building, all under one roof, will probably consume less energy. A compact multi-storied facility will be the most energy efficient in terms of shape. Some suggest that a circular shape is especially good for conserving energy.

5. Building Orientation

The location of the building on the site affects energy consumption. Energy will be saved if the position of the building provides for the best utilization of and protection from the sun and wind. For example, buildings in southeast Florida oriented to expose windows and doors to the east and/or south will benefit from the eastern and southern prevailing breezes of the summer. Such breezes will help cool the facility. During the winter, the cool air and sometimes cold winds come from the west and north. Therefore, the building should have a minimum of windows on the building's north and west sides.

6. Natural Ground Features

All the natural ground features of the site should be considered as potential allies in energy conservation. Trees, shrubs and berms are potential helpers in saving energy. Trees and shrubs can be used to break cold northern winds and keep them from reaching the surface of the north-facing walls. Existing or constructed berms can be of similar assistance. There is no better insulator than "Mother Earth". Windows in east walls, and especially in the west walls, need protection from the direct rays of the sun. Sunlight passing through windows generates considerable heat. Trees and large shrubs can be used to shield these windows from the direct rays of the summer sun.

7. Windows

The use of exterior windows should be balanced between the potential for facilitating the movement of air and the potential for heat loss and gain. When windows are used, they should be protected from the direct rays of the sun, and/or should be double-glazed or made to reflect the sun's rays. To avoid the closed-in feeling that can come from having dark windows or windows high on the wall (clerestory), the interior of the building can be constructed with fewer or shorter walls in some areas. Indirect lighting can also be used to correct this problem.

8. Lighting

Although lights do not consume as much energy as heating and air-conditioning units, they do consume their share and should be considered during the planning stages. Whenever possible, fluorescent lights should be used rather than incandescent. Incandescent bulbs produce much more heat than fluorescent tubes as well as being less energy efficient. The additional heat from the incandescent bulbs will have to be removed from the facility in the summer via increased air conditioning, exhaust fans, or other ventilation equipment.

For parking lots, some high intensity discharge lamps are extremely efficient and provide greater lumens in comparison to certain mercury lamps. Their color may not always be to our liking, but the energy saving is considerable in comparison to lamps with more traditional color. Some rooms should be equipped with multiple light switches controlling rows or banks of fixtures. Lights next to windows should be controlled by one switch with others controlled by other switches. If there are two or more entrances to a room, each entry/exit should have a light switch(es). These light switches could be the kind that sense the presence of people and automatically turn on, and turn off when people leave the room.

Timers should be installed for all outside lights to avoid having someone forget to turn them off.

Finally, arrangements should be made for the use of natural light. This can be done by placing some windows high in the wall (clerestory). These windows can be shaded from the direct rays of the sun by a roof overhang or some designed "eyebrow," and still allow indirect lighting.

9. Mechanical Design

More energy-efficient air conditioners, heaters, pumps, fans and other mechanical equipment are now available as compared to previous decades.

The selection, location, and proper installation is the responsibility of experts who are able to analyze and predict airflow, cost factors, and final energy consumption. Their help is vital to the design and construction of an energy-efficient educational facility.

10. Computers

Computerized control of air-conditioning, ventilation, humidity, heating and lighting can conserve energy. A properly programmed computer can help maintain room temperature levels no matter how many or how few people are present, monitor timing devices, detect equipment problems and control the heating of water for restrooms and kitchens. Of course, the saving of energy is also affected by the equipment described in Number 9 above, and the attitude toward energy conservation of the people using the facility. Computers can also be used to provide information about energy use that should be helpful in the analysis of energy expenditures in an energy conservation program.

Appendix C is a building survey form that can be used to help the committee become more sensitive to building energy conservation. It can provide the committee members with the practice that is needed when attempting to translate theory into practice.

An Energy Conservation Program

The educational facility planning committee should make a note to suggest an ongoing energy conservation program to those who will eventually manage the facility. Such a program could include the following ideas:

1.   Provide Energy Conservation Programs for Maintenance Personnel

Obviously, _people_ make a facility energy efficient. Energy devices are of little use when not used or when bypassed by users who do not agree with the setting on the controls or who are simply energy lazy. One way to prevent this problem is to invite users and maintenance personnel to help plan the energy conservation program and to be involved in its administration. Another way is to plan an incentive procedure whereby dollars saved, or some fraction, are placed in the general fund of the facility. Occasional surveys, requests for advice and general meetings to discuss energy issues are strong invitations for users to become "owners" of the system and to strongly support its goals.

2.   Establish an On-Going Preventative Maintenance Program

Record books should be designed to record periodic equipment checks. These records should indicate the routine maintenance to be performed, observations to be made, and provide proper check-off space, including date of work performed, for each piece of equipment. Such records should be maintained in a central and highly visible location. A computer program could be written that will indicate what and when maintenance should be performed.

3. Plan for the Periodic Evaluation of Energy Usage

Building administrators need to meet with maintenance personnel for periodic inspection of energy-use records. Increases in energy consumption must be analyzed and, if possible, a determination made as to the source of this increase. The entire conservation program is of little use if no monitoring takes place, or the information obtained from monitoring is not used to encourage additional conservation, or to maintain the existing level of energy consumption.

4. Upgrade the Energy System as New Technology Develops

Greater savings might be possible when new equipment comes on the market. Monitoring such innovations through subscriptions to professional journals and contact with architects/engineers, state agencies and local universities will help keep the energy conservation system at its maximum potential. Knowing the energy efficiency ratings of equipment, as noted in the equipment log, will make possible a quick comparison with the new technology.

REFERENCES

Wilson, Marian L. (1981). Environmental considerations for learning environments. In Phillip J. Sleeman & D. M. Rockwell (Eds.), <u>Designing learning environments</u> (p. 93). New York: Longman Inc.

<u>The economy of energy conservation in educational facilities</u>. New York: Educational Facilities Laboratories, p. 2.

Neill, Shirley Boes (1977). <u>School energy crisis: Problems and solutions</u>. VA: Educational News Service for American Association of School Administration, p. 9.

CHAPTER 5

VANDALISM DESIGN CONSIDERATIONS

In planning an educational facility, it is practical and economical to consider the problem of vandalism. Planning for the prevention of vandalism is practical because the damage done can cause a serious disruption of the activities that were to take place in the facility. It is also economical simply because of the cost of repairing broken windows, doors, ceiling tiles, bathroom fixtures and other parts of the building.

Vandalism is certainly an old problem. Writers in the American Colonial era occasionally described schools that were damaged by vandals. As the years have gone by and the size, number and complexity of educational buildings increased, the value of property exposed to vandals likewise increased.

The attitudes of the people in the community toward the facility and its personnel seem to be related to the facility's vandalism potential (Young, 1970). Generally speaking, communities that take pride in their school enjoy lower rates of school property destruction. Additionally, communities which perceive their schools as aesthetically pleasing tend to regard them with an enhanced sense of pride.

Previous chapters have encouraged considerable involvement from the community, and from agencies serving this community, in order to ensure that all citizens know they can use the facility when it is completed. Involvement also was encouraged in order for the planning committee to have access to a wide range of ideas from the general public and government agencies. This involvement will also contribute to a lessening of vandalism potential; once open, the potential will continue to be reduced as long as the facility serves the needs of the community.

Involving the community in the planning stage of the educational facility will invite community pride in the final product. If the planning steps described in previous chapters have been followed, the planning committee is well on its way toward the prevention of acts of vandalism in the new facility.

Defining Vandalism

Defining vandalism is important. It is important because damage occurs to a facility for a variety of reasons. Some damage is caused by the improper use of equipment. Windows are sometimes broken during the playing of ball games. Occasionally, someone may break into a facility and destroy equipment. To call all this vandalism is to confuse the reason for the expenditure of funds to repair the facility or replace broken equipment. When administrators do not fully understand problems, they obviously are not likely to come to a reasonable solution.

The American Association of School Administrators published "Stopping School Property Damage" in 1976 (Ziesel, 1976). In this publication, four types of damage to buildings are defined. These definitions were devised in order to sort damage into specific categories. Such categories make possible a better analysis of the building damage than when all damage is listed in one category. (See Table 3)

Ziesel divided damage to buildings into four categories:

1. Malicious damage that requires immediate attention, such as broken doors caused by someone attempting to break into the facility

2. Deliberate, but non-malicious, damage that requires repair, but which can be done at a convenient time in the future, such as repainting a wall upon which people have attached notices, ads, announcements or other items, the removal of which, causes the wall paint to also be removed.

3. Accidental damage that requires immediate attention such as a broken fire alarm box caused when someone was moving a large box down a hallway

4. Accidental damage that will require eventual repair, such as damage to shrubs from cars where the shrubs were planted too close to the parking spaces

The above scheme for sorting damage allows the administrator to separate out routine wear and tear on the building from the cost of malicious vandalism. This is important, since recurring damage to the same equipment or building material suggests the need for replacement with something much more resistant to damage, rather than a concern with vandalism, which requires a different reaction.

Malicious damage and deliberate but non-malicious damage could be combined into one category. In this way, record keeping is a little more simple, and the basic concern for understanding why damage occurs can remain foremost in our thinking.

Keeping an accurate record of damage in the four categories might entail more work as compared to lumping all damage together, but a large educational facility, used by thousands of community residents, demands accurate record keeping. A computerized accounting procedure might be used.

Table 3

Property Damage Described in Terms of Motive and Consequences of Damage

| | CONSEQUENCE | |
MOTIVE	Instantaneous Damage Demanding Immediate Attention	Cumulative Damage Demanding Eventual Attention
Conscious	Malicious Vandalism .	Non-Malicious Property Damage
Not Purposeful	Misnamed Vandalism	Hidden Maintenance Damage

Note. From "Stopping School Property Damage" (p. 11) by J. Zeisel, 1976, Arlington, VA: American Association of School Administrators and Educational Facilities Laboratory. Copyright 1976 by John Zeisel. Reprinted by permission.

Social Considerations

"Social considerations" is defined as the manner in which the facility personnel respond to the needs of the community.

When the educational facility is completely ready for occupancy, the physical considerations designed to prevent or reduce property damage will still not prevent property damage from occurring on the site. The installation of tamper-proof screws, hard-use equipment and hard, smooth surfaces will tend to lower routine maintenance costs as well as reduce opportunities for vandalism. But vandalism can occur in spite of the best of physical design considerations. The reduction of vandalism and the lowering of routine maintenance costs can occur as a result of both design considerations and social considerations.

When conscious or malicious vandalism begins, an assessment of the manner in which administrative, service, and teaching personnel are relating to the participants is in order. In addition, the relationship between the programs offered and the needs of the surrounding community should be reviewed. It may be that at least one of these two needs improvement. An exception might be the sudden one-time damage of the facility by vandals who have come for the excitement inherent in causing damage. If the facility is serving the needs of the community, both programmatically and interpersonally, then this isolated incident of damage to the facility should not continue on a regular basis.

Those with a teaching role in the facility can act to prevent vandalism by designing lesson plans that invite all learners to be successful. Those students who are successful in learning will probably be satisfied with their attempts at learning. Those who are satisfied while learning in the facility will probably perceive the facility as a pleasant place to be. Those who enjoy the facility are not likely to deliberately damage it.

The same actions that teachers initiate toward building guests, can be asked of support personnel and administrators. All facility personnel should be concerned about preventing vandalism and routine wear on the facility. Support personnel and administrators can implement this concern by viewing community requests for their assistance as opportunities to serve and help. Smiling and treating questions from community participants with respect will invite participant behavior that respects the facility personnel and the facility itself. Constantly evaluating program offerings against current community needs is a must.

Lastly, these social considerations imply hiring personnel with special interpersonal skills in the first place. Such people should be able to point out in their employment applications specific behavior in their past that demonstrates a willingness to serve those whose tax dollars ultimately pay the facility staff salaries.

Physical Design Considerations

There are several areas of a building that seem to suffer more property damage than others. Whether remodeling a used building or designing a new one, the following areas will need special care:

1. Grounds and Exterior Walls

A facility that is pleasing to the eye seems to suffer less malicious and non-malicious vandalism. Painted exterior walls, curving walkways, plenty of trees and shrubs, and rolling grounds seem pleasant and inviting. Maintenance for this type of exterior space is high; however, financial savings from a reduction in vandalism costs could be budgeted for funding this maintenance cost.

Use non-toxic shrubbery that is flexible, grows rapidly and does not produce berries or seeds which can cause problems in and of themselves. Keep shrubbery low when planted near the building, thereby eliminating hiding places. Keep shrubbery away from parking lot areas where car doors will damage them upon opening.

Consider installing only a few sidewalks at first in order to let pedestrian traffic determine the best location for the remaining walkways needed.

For play areas, provide equipment able to withstand hard play. Keep lights, windows and shrubbery away from such areas if the play is likely to cause them damage. For large, windowless walls, arrange for the painting of tennis nets or batting or strike zones on these walls. This arrangement will facilitate playing in approved areas. Play sometimes occurs on weekends, evenings or during certain summer hours in unapproved areas. Try to change the unapproved areas to approved ones by protecting windows with screens, and protect shrubbery with low, solid walls placed between the shrubbery and the playing area.

First floor windows should be extra strong or protected to withstand breakage. Consideration should be given to use of the harder plastics to protect upper floor windows. Doors, too, will need to be well built, with the area by the panic bar hidden by opaque panels so outsiders trying to break in cannot actually see the bar. Try not to design the doorway as a recessed area. Such a doorway provides a potential hiding area.

Keep trees and electrical/telephone poles from being installed next to buildings. They provide climbing paths to the roof. If area lights are attached to the exterior wall, try to recess them or cover them with unbreakable covers.

2.   Ceilings, Walls, and Floors

Many school facilities have acoustical tile on the ceilings of corridors. If these ceilings are low, they attract marks from a variety of writing instruments, and can be broken when hit by those walking below. The goal of the ceiling covering is sound suppression and to provide a covering for the above pipes and wiring. Two other possibilities exist to accomplish the same goals: carpeting on walls and/or floors made from a variety of colored threads, and hard surfaces (plaster) for the ceiling. This two part combination might be sufficient for noise suppression, screening and vandalism reduction. The second is to simply raise the ceiling, thereby keeping the tiles above jumping height for the average pedestrian.

Walls tend to become writing surfaces. Covering the wall surface with carpet is one way to handle the situation. This solution also carries with it a different problem--occasional cleaning. Another possibility is to paint the wall with a paint that dries very hard. The wall can be either very smooth or covered with a fine pebble texture. A smooth surface can be too smooth for many writing materials.

Walls designed with indentations where two or three people can gather is not a good idea as far as vandalism is concerned. Wherever possible, corridors should be without these areas. This same rule applies to other areas such as entryways, exits and the top and bottom of stairs. Where elimination of such gathering places is not possible, the designers must expect the occasional gathering of groups in these areas and, therefore, the need to strengthen these areas in regard to heating/cooling vents, doors or windows, and ceilings.

Floors are usually hard surface tiles, seamless coverings or carpet. Carpet has a sound suppression quality and seems pleasant to walk upon. The harder surfaces are less susceptible to vandalism, but afford no acoustical quality.

3. Restrooms

Walls should be painted with a hard and very smooth paint. The ceiling should be treated in a similar manner, including an unbreakable surface. Stall partitions should be attached to structural members of the wall with special attachments that cannot be removed without special tools. Sinks should be cast iron and wall mounted. The mounting bracket should be heavy duty steel and bolted to the support beams in the wall. Soap dispensers should be of the central type with only the dispenser valve visible. Mirrors should be either metal or plastic.

Attractive hand washing areas might be constructed outside the restrooms. The place-ment of this type of equipment outside the restroom reduces the amount of unobserved time. Hand washing equipment used in industrial plants would not be acceptable, since it tends to invite a factory atmosphere.

Restrooms could be constructed without exit and entrance doors. Screening walls can be designed to provide the required privacy. If located outside the restroom, wash bowls, mirrors and soap dispensers can then be observed from the hallway.

The condition of restrooms is frequently viewed by the public as an indication of the respect participants have for the building and the programs housed there. Physical plant design considerations coupled with social considerations that mitigate against vandalism will be needed to keep restrooms in a condition that will communicate a cleanliness and attractiveness pleasing to the public.

4. Miscellaneous

Fire alarm stations should be used only where required by law. For instance, several states require pull stations only in areas where the seating capacity exceeds fifty occupants. Whenever possible, smoke detectors should be used in lieu of pull stations.

The planners might also consider a fire warning system that rings only in the administrative offices (if allowed by state law/regulation). Once an administrator has concluded that public fire fighting services are needed, the fire alarm system is then allowed to complete its process of ringing throughout the building and in the local fire station.

Thermostats should be located in areas out of reach of passing pedestrians and should have vandal-proof covers. State code will suggest their placement in rooms.

REFERENCES

Young, George & Soldatis, Stephen (June 1970). School vandalism can be stopped. American School and University, 42, 23.

Ziesel, John (1976). Stopping school property damage. Arlington, VA: American Association of School Administrators and Educational Facilities Laboratory.

CHAPTER 6

TECHNOLOGY

If you had the responsibility to design the area
of a building which would provide for the automated
office/classroom, how would you proceed in order to
accommodate all current and future possibilities?
Since most of us are new to the idea of the automated
office/classroom, we might have some difficulty
designing the technical aspects--such as wiring and
the type of floors and walls required for housing large
computers. We could, however, recommend a process
whereby the technological requirements and human needs
of the occupants of such an educational facility would
probably be met. We would at least hope to increase
beyond mere chance the possibility for meeting such
needs.

The purpose of this chapter is to suggest a
planning strategy, and to inform the reader about some
of the physical requirements of current technology.
This is done in the hope of assisting the planning team
in its task of developing a human resource facility
that meets the needs of those to be served by this
facility.

Hardware, People, and Environment

Hardware, people, and environment are the three
basic factors in planning for the automated
office/classroom. Integrating these factors to promote
efficiency, effectiveness and personal satisfaction is
the challenge. "For the very first time, planning for
new machines and planning for new facilities must be
integrated" (Pulgram, 1984).

The hardware, people and environment factors are:

1. Hardware

A. Wiring: providing for cable TV, computer
to computer communications (city-to-city tele-

55

communications), inter-office sharing of a large computer, inter-office communicating (net-working), monitoring of equipment (lights, heating, air-conditioning, security devices)

B.   Machines and the workspace: integrating these two in order to increase availability, ease of work, and keeping the machines (computers, printers, television and radio sets) from being obtrusive

C.   Seating: selected for comfort, utility and contribution to the building's aesthetic ambience

D.   Lighting: non-glare, the elimination of shadows, proper intensity

E.   Room and building flexibility: ease of workspace, wall and equipment movement, expandability or contractability, accessibility, adaptability

2.   People

A.   Seating: see above

B.   Privacy: offices designed to provide some sense of privacy for the employee

C.   Communication: offices designed to pro-vide ease of communication between employee and clients as well as other employees

D.   Personal space: a recognition of the personal need for space to store personal belongings and current work

3.   Environment

A.   Safety and security: a need basic to all humans

B.   Communication: physical traffic flow and inter-personal communication facilitated by color schemes, corridor design, placement of signs, placement of equipment

C.   Aesthetic ambience: the use of lighting, colors, texture, communication patterns, and type of building signs that invite a personal sense of comfort, security and satisfaction

56

D. Space: space is not simply a matter of
necessity to accommodate physical needs of
people and equipment. The manner in which
people perceive space is also an important
consideration. Planners must attempt to provide
psychological space.   Psychological space is
that space left open between equipment and
personal work space that, by its mere existence,
invites people to perceive the space as
comforting, inviting, spacious, and available
for informal conversations. The planning team
might visit existing offices and classrooms and
hold brief conversations about the spaciousness
or lack of spaciousness with the occupants in
order to better plan the new facility.

The Planning Process

This process, as with the processes previously
discussed, is characterized by widespread involvement
of those affected by technology in the office or
classroom. The process should provide for involvement
by the architect, owners/leaseholder and clients.
With effective leadership, this involvement should lead
to a good plan for the current and future use of
technology in the educational facility.

Step One: General committee orientation.
Discussions at this meeting should cover such topics as
the general purpose of this committee, how this
committee's work fits into the general scheme that is
to produce an educational facility, who is to be
involved in the committee's work, how the committee
will make decisions, and to whom the committee is to
report.

Step Two: Action plan. Once the task has been
identified and understood by all committee members, an
action plan can be developed. Such a plan will include
a step-by-step procedure for completing the task,
designate who will be responsible for each step of the
plan, describe materials and other resources required
for each step, and establish its due date. Copies of
this plan should be distributed to all committee
members as well as to the general planning committee's
chairperson.

Step Three: Data collection. Data should be
collected from clients, owners/leaseholders, and

technology experts. Information needed will revolve around the anticipated kinds of automation required in order to meet client needs in an effective and efficient manner. Information will be gathered regarding the kinds of automation required for the agency offices, as well as the kind of equipment required to meet client learning needs. Included in the data collection will be information on the number and kinds of handicapped clients to be served by this educational facility. Such information will impact on the kinds of computers and other equipment purchased, and the location and availability of this technology to facilitate the satisfaction of handicapped client needs.

Step Four: Data organization. Once the data has been collected, the committee should organize it into organizational needs, group needs, and individual needs. The data collection process might include trying to collect the data in this fashion; however, such a process tends to restrict the freedom of those supplying the data when required to think along these lines. In any case, the data will have to be reviewed to be sure all data is in the correct category. Obviously, some data can appear on more than one list.

Step Five: Data analysis. In this process, the committee will look for connections or relationships between organizational, individual and group needs. This determination will help the experts and architect decide the placement of lines of communication: telephone lines, computer lines, electrical outlets, cable TV lines, pedestrian walkways, antennas, and other such communication elements. The analysis will also help in determining the location of personal spaces/work-stations, technological equipment, tele-conference rooms, automation equipment for the handicapped, and rooms to house large computers.

Step Six: Final report. This report generally includes a statement as to how the group obtained its data and otherwise came to its conclusions. The conclusions or recommendations to the general education planning committee could come at the beginning or the end of the report. A very careful review and editing of the final report will increase its readability and chances for complete communication.

Technical Considerations

Does the installation of a mainframe computer and

microcomputers require special wiring, security, or placement? What special procedures and other arrangements will be needed when computers are used for instruction?

No one on the planning committee is expected to be an expert on office automation, computer assisted instruction, or telecommunications. But to have no idea at all of the technical factors necessary for today's technology would be to place all technology decisions in the hands of those outside the planning group. Such circumstances are a bit risky because the experts tend not to challenge their own assumptions thereby limiting creativity. If the planning group has at least some basic information about technology, they might ask some challenging questions that result in even better office automation, computer-assisted instruction, and telecommunication designs. The following brief description of some of the basic considerations for installing technological equipment is offered to help the planning committee become a bit more knowledgeable than might otherwise be the case.

Mainframe (computer with a large storage capacity)

1. After purchasing the mainframe computer, be prepared to buy more equipment. You cannot provide for the maximum amount of possible use since there is no way to determine the maximum at the beginning of a computer project. The best you can do is guess at the use level needed for the near future and be prepared to add on later.

2. You must arrange for the installation of static-free flooring. Since most computers use only a very small amount of voltage, a charge of static electricity from your finger to a poorly grounded computer could destroy some of the micro-chips. Result: loss of computer time, a hole in your computer budget.

3. Fire-fighting equipment should include ceiling, under floor and hand-held extinguishers. This equipment must provide a gas element type of extinguisher rather than ones that contain water or dry particles to extinguish any fires. Of course, water cannot be used on electrical equipment and dry particles may damage the equipment when they coat circuit boards and other parts. "Halon" is the trade name for this type of gas element

extinguisher. This gas is part of the Freon family of gases, and can be purchased commercially as "1301" for the under floor and ceiling type of system, and "1211" for the portable extinguisher.

4. Provision for electrical surge protection must be included in the building design. Any sudden increase in volts (such as can occur during electrical storms or during other alterations in the current to your building) can damage the computers.

5. Conditioned air is required for the mainframe computer room. Room temperature must be regulated so the room temperature does not rise above 80 degrees Fahrenheit. Humidity should be 80 percent or less. The reason for these parameters is to prevent corrosion of parts in the computer or the coating of parts with moisture that might eventually short circuit the system. Additionally, the mainframe computer, and to a much lesser extent the microcomputers, generate heat which needs to be removed in order to preserve the units. Besides the need to remove heat and prevent the accumulation of moisture, the conditioned air requirement is necessary to prevent <u>sudden</u> changes in temperature. These changes will cause metals of different properties to expand or contract, thereby causing breakage over time.

6. The machinery that provides the conditioned air should be on its own electrical circuit with an automatic back-up generator. Loss of air conditioning could require a rapid shut-down of the mainframe. Such a quick shut-down could mean the loss of data from the memory units or damage to software because the computer operator might not have enough time to follow the correct procedure for shutting down the computers. With a separate circuit and back-up generator, those monitoring the computers can arrange for a normal shut-down thus protecting the data in storage and the software programs.

7. The air conditioning unit should be equip- ped with a dust-filtering system and given regular maintenance. Increased dust in the air increases the chance for data loss or damage to software.

8. A water seepage alarm system is needed to indicate the presence of water on the floor. Without the alarm, the accumulating water could cause electrical short circuits before anyone realizes water is present. Such a problem can damage the mainframe as well as cause the loss of data and damage software.

9. Plan for the construction of a false floor (commonly called a "computer floor") that is raised about twelve inches above the support floor. The area between the floors can be used for all the connecting wires and cool air circulation (large computers are usually designed to take in cool air from the floor area).

10. Try to purchase equipment manufactured after October 1983. A new federal standard on noise radiation (the radiation of electronic waves from each unit) came into effect at that time. Electronic noise can cause interference when putting in or taking out data from the computer.

11. Because of the sound of fans in the computers and the noise from the printers, the room housing the mainframe should have sound suppression material applied to the walls and ceiling.

12. Indirect lighting should be used to reduce glare and reflections on the screens of the monitors.

13. Security should be provided for the computer area where very expensive equipment is located. Security should be both physical and human. Physical security includes locks, bars, doors, and removal of windows to name a few. Human security would require having someone in the area to monitor those who enter. Access to a telephone and an alarm button to signal for assistance are necessary.

14. Be sure all information stored on tapes or disks is copied onto a second tape or disk. Extra copies should be stored in a nearby but separate area safe from possible destruction should the original be destroyed. This storage area should be properly secured, and air conditioned.

15. Be generous in the installation of 110 volt electrical outlets. Flexibility is needed in the mainframe room and a large number of outlets will provide for some of this needed flexibility.

16. An uninterrupted power supply (UPS) should be provided. This is a very expensive installation but is necessary.

Microcomputers

The rooms to house microcomputers for teaching/learning also have special requirements to be considered during construction. These requirements are not as extensive as those discussed above, but are just as important considering the expense and effort involved in the original purchase.

1. Non-static flooring is required here, too. Electrical contact between people and equipment could cause damage to the computer.

2. These rooms should be equipped with a large number of 110 volt duplex outlets. Flexibility is the key. In coming years, newer equipment will be available that might require a different arrangement of the units.

3. Provide an unobstructed view of the entire room for the person who is to monitor the activities. This will tend to reduce the number of monitors needed.

4. Because some terminals will be connected directly to printers or the mainframe computer, the distance between rooms must be considered. All equipment comes with manufacturer specifications concerning the maximum distance allowed for such connections.

5. Include plenty of bulletin board space in these rooms for notices, offers of help from other learners, and other related information. Standard chalkboards should be excluded because the dust from erasing can slowly work its way into the computer and begin to coat circuit boards and other computer parts. Such coating might cause problems with the computer

operation.

6. Include some plain tables in these rooms for studying printouts. It is a waste of other's time (and the district's funds which were used to purchase the computers) to look for programming errors in one's program while displayed on the terminal rather than using study tables.

7. Purchase one printer for every three or four terminals. These printers are in addition to the one(s) used in connection with the mainframe computer.

8. Software (disks for storing data and program disks which instruct the computer how to respond to your commands) must be stored and handled in a secure manner. Handing out software program disks to learners increases the chance for damage and theft. A better way to let others use these computer programs might be to place them on hard disks. Hard disks are disks which never leave the disk drive. Terminal users could then access those drives under the control of the room monitor and electronically insert them into the memory bank of their terminal. Check copyright laws first.

9. The purchase of different models of computers should be limited to as few as possible. The more models, the more difficult to find experts with the knowledge for using, maintaining and instructing on these different computers.

The Management Process

Just as important as the facilities for the hardware and software is the process for managing the entire project. Here are a few management suggestions you might want to consider as you plan for the installation and use of this new teaching and administration tool.

1. Set some teaching/learning terminals aside for ten-minute use only. Some users will need only a few minutes to make a simple correction to their program. Making them wait an hour for access to a terminal would not be fair.

2. Recruit a few experts to provide immediate assistance to terminal users. One expert in the room at a time should be sufficient unless the terminals are being used for formal instruction.

3. Develop an advisory committee to make recommendations about purchases and the operation of the system. Local amateurs, computer club members, users of the system, experts from local business and others would make good members of such a committee.

4. If possible, develop separate teaching and general use areas. Once the system is operational, use will grow and the two areas will be needed.

5. Develop a documentation library. Documents are the manuals that provide an explanation of the operation of the equipment, update programs, and explain the software use procedures. Signing out these documents to users will not prevent the removal of selected pages. As a classroom project, put these documents onto a disk and let users access the disk like they would software--see Number 8 above. There can be no theft, damage or wear with such a method. Caution: These books are copyrighted. Check with the manufacturer before proceeding.

Computers can be used as tools in the process of improving service to the community. With proper preparation for the installation of the equipment, the development of management procedures, and adequate training of all who will use the equipment, these tools can help attain the goal of making the community a better place to live.

REFERENCES

Pulgram, William L., & Stonis, Richard E. (1984). <u>Designing the automated office</u>, New York: Whitney Library of Design, p. 7.

CHAPTER 7

RESOURCES

Additional information is available for each of the chapter topics as listed below. Some of the information provides an additional explanation of the topic. In some cases worksheets or simulations have been furnished for committee chairpersons or groups to use in generating additional data or to provide a more structured involvement of others. For some chapters, people or organizations are listed who can provide expert advice.

CHAPTER 1 A Planning Process

1. Most states have Centers for Community Education located in universities and state departments of education. These centers frequently have some expertise in the development of prioritized needs, determination of resources, and the encouragement of cooperation among governmental units, social agencies and other organizations interested in the broad field of education. Addresses and telephone numbers of these centers are available through the state departments of education.

2. The Charles Stewart Mott Foundation
1200 Mott Foundation Building
Flint, Michigan 48502-1851
(313)238-5651

The Foundation is interested in a variety of human concerns including the development of social service agency/schools cooperation, government/schools partnerships, and other related issues. They also can furnish the addresses for Centers for Community Education.

3. National Community Education Association
119 North Payne Street
Alexandria, Virginia 22314, (703)683-NCEA

The NCEA publishes the Community Education

Journal. Volume VII, Number 2, January 1980, focuses on educational facilities. Volume VIII, Number 2, January 1981 has a special section on cooperative relationships. Request information on other issues that include articles on facilities.

4. Council of Educational Facility Planners, Int'l.
   29 West Woodruff Avenue
   Columbus, Ohio 43210

In the late 70's and early 80's, the Council published some pamphlets about the planning and construction of educational facilities. Some of these pamphlets may still be available.

The Council is also the publisher of the "Community Planning Assistance Kit." This kit contains a general planning process, designed for the use of citizens and agencies working together for the improvement of their communities. While it was not developed for the designing of educational facilities, it is an excellent general planning guide that can be adopted by those interested in facilities.

5. Educational Facilities Laboratories
   850 Third Avenue
   New York, N.Y. 10022

This organization has a variety of publications about educational facilities. They have an excellent six-part series entitled, "Community School Centers". Each is 25 or 30 pages in length. They may also have other publications available.

6. American Association of School Administrators
   1801 North Moore Street
   Arlington, Virginia 22209

AASA has published several pamphlets about school facilities.

7. Perspectives on the Group Process, edited by C. Gilbert Wrenn and C. Gratton Kemp
   Houghton Mifflin Company, Boston, 1964.

Several chapters are especially good. See Part

Three: The Group Process, Part Four: Leadership, and Part Five: The Group Member.

8. Cooperative Extension Service
    Iowa State University
    Ames, Iowa 50011

The Cooperative Extension Service of the U.S. Department of Agriculture has a number of publications about the skills needed by members of planning groups. They also have a slide/tape program entitled, "Creating Coordination Among Organizations." This approach to coordination is quite unusual, in that it provides for maintaining the original concern of the initiating agency while facilitating coordination among several agencies.

9. Educational Improvement Center
    207 Delsea Drive (Rt. 47)
    Sewell, New Jersey 08080

The Educational Improvement Center has produced a packet called, "The Art of the Impossible: School-Municipal Cooperation." It contains a slide/tape, research on cooperation, a guide for planning, and material for the printing of overhead transparencies.

10. Phi Delta KAPPAN
    February 1984

The theme of this issue is, "Building Links Between Schools and Communities." All six articles on this topic support the notion that schools can be improved if families, businesses and the general citizenry develop a much stronger link with their schools. These articles will provide a good background for community leaders who wish to develop a cooperative relationship between community and school in the planning of educational facilities.

11. The National Elementary PRINCIPAL
    Volume 54, Number 3, January/February 1975

This issue of the Principal has nine articles on the theme of "The Ecology of Education: Community." All of these articles are excellent beginnings to the understanding of the need for cooperation between citizens and the agencies created to serve them.

12. <u>Appendix</u> <u>A</u> of this publication is an instruction sheet for a simulation called, Community Dilemma. This simulation is an excellent tool to help the members of planning committees learn about working together. It involves dividing the group into subgroups and inviting them to solve problems. When the activity is followed by a debriefing period to discuss the behavior of the groups, the benefits of working together and how to accomplish this become obvious to the group members.

<u>CHAPTER</u> <u>2</u> <u>Beginning</u> <u>With</u> <u>Function</u> <u>Rather</u> <u>Than</u> <u>Form</u>

1. Clearing House
    December 1971, Volume 46, Number 4

This journal contains a self test entitled, "What is Your EP? A test which identifies your educational philosophy." The self test provides an interesting point for the discussion of various educational philosophies.

<u>CHAPTER</u> <u>3</u> <u>Meeting</u> <u>Community</u> <u>Needs</u>

Several books and pamphlets are available on the topic of resource and needs assessment. A few are listed below.

1. <u>Community</u> <u>Analysis:</u> <u>Getting</u> <u>to</u> <u>Know</u> <u>Your</u> <u>Community</u>, by Beaulieu, Pyle, Korsching, and Carter. Available from the Institute of Food and Agricultural Sciences, University of Florida, Gainesville, Florida, 32601.

2. <u>Assessing</u> <u>Your</u> <u>Community</u>, by Marc R. Levy. Available from the Northwest Community Education Development Center, University of Oregon, 1724 Moss Street, Eugene, Oregon 97403.

3. <u>A</u> <u>Guide</u> <u>to</u> <u>Needs</u> <u>Assessment</u> <u>in</u> <u>Community</u> <u>Education</u>, Superintendent of Documents, U. S. Government Printing Office, Washington, D.C. 20402.

4. <u>Assessing</u> <u>the</u> <u>Educationally</u> <u>Related</u> <u>Needs</u> <u>of</u> <u>Adults:</u> <u>A</u> <u>Practical,</u> <u>Low</u> <u>Cost</u> <u>Approach</u>, by Sandra C. Grady, American Association of Community and Junior Colleges, Washington, D.C.

5. <u>An</u> <u>Overview</u> <u>to</u> <u>Community</u> <u>Need/Resource</u> <u>Assessment</u>, by Dr. Augustus Little, Stewart Mott Davis Center for Community Education, University of Florida, Gainesville, Florida 32601.

6. <u>Translating</u> <u>needs</u> <u>to</u> <u>design:</u> Once the needs of the people who will use the facility have been determined, the needs must be translated into activities or conditions that will satisfy the needs. Once the activities or conditions have been described, the committee can determine their implications for the design of the educational facility. <u>Appendix</u> <u>B</u> is an example of this process.

CHAPTER 4 Energy Use Considerations

1. CEFP Journal, May-June, 1986, Vol. 24, No. 3.

This issue of the CEFP Journal contains a variety of articles on energy conservation. Other issues also contain information about energy conservation and many other issues important to educational facility planners. The Journal is available at $25.00 per year from Council of Educational Facility Planners, International, 29 W. Woodruff Ave., Columbus, Ohio 43210.

2. <u>Appendix</u> <u>C</u> is a energy conservation survey instrument. Only a light meter and thermometer are needed to complete the form. Using it to perform a survey of a facility will help the user gain experience in planning this phase of a new facility.

CHAPTER 5 Vandalism Design Considerations

1. Probably the best book about vandalism prevention has been published by the American Association of School Administrators and Educational Facilities Laboratories, in

collaboration with the City of Boston Public Facilities Department. It is especially valuable because it begins with a discussion of the meaning of vandalism and how prevention of vandalism is primarily a social matter and, only secondarily, a physical design strategy.

Chapter Two examines exterior design strategies and chapter three looks at interior strategies. The book concludes with chapters on administrative responses and design account- ability checklists.

CHAPTER 6 Technology

Hundreds of books and magazines have now been published on technology and education. Most public and school professional libraries have the necessary background material in order to acquaint the planners with this aspect of the educational facility design process.

Since the goal of educational technology designs is the improved effectiveness of learning and work in the educational facility, it would be appropriate for the planners to begin their study of technology with some reading about the intended interaction between technology and students/teachers. Educational Leadership, Volume 43, Number 6, March 1986, has a special section entitled, "Empowering Students and Teachers Through Technology." These sixteen articles should provide a good background for most types of educational technology.

APPENDICES

DIRECTIONS FOR THE USE OF COMMUNITY DILEMMA

Purpose: To invite participants to experience opportunities for small group cooperation or conflict.

Process: 1. Explain to participants that they are invited to participate in a simulation about how groups work together. This process will involve dividing the group into several small groups, and presenting each with a small problem to solve. Instructions will be handed out to each group.

2. Group facilitator divides group into several small groups of about five or six each. Seat groups with enough space between them so they can have some privacy when doing their work. At least three such groups are needed for the process to be successful.

3. Facilitator distributes one copy of the Community Dilemma Guide Sheet to each group. Group is then asked to share the information among all group members.

4. After groups have read through the Guide Sheet, the facilitator then briefly explains the process.

A. Each group will be given two cards; one marked with an "A" and the other with a "B".

B. Each group is to decide whether to hold up an "A" card or a "B" card for the first round keeping in mind the objective of Community Dilemma as explained in the Guide Sheet. As facilitator, do not attempt to explain anything further about the objective of the simulation, such as this is an experience to test your ability to cooperate or manage inter-group conflict.

C. Each group is to decide whether to hold up an "A" card or a "B" card for each of the remaining rounds as they are called by the facilitator. The Guide Sheet calls for five minutes between each round. This frequently is more time than is needed, especially in the later rounds.

D. The facilitator will post for all to see the results of each round.

5. Ask each group to decide upon a name for their group so you do not have to address each with numbers, or "Hey you!". (This will assist the group to develop a group cohesiveness. Dividing the participants into groups will also assist in this process.)

6. Prepare on a large chalkboard or pieces of newsprint a chart on which to keep score after each round. Place the group names across the top and the eight rounds down the left side.

7. Instruct the groups that, for round one, they now have five minutes during which to decide as a group whether to hold up an "A" or "B" card. Instruct the groups to hold up their cards when called for by the facilitator.

8. Resist telling the groups how to play the game. If asked questions about the process, shrug your shoulders, or ask them to decide. All the information to be given out by the facilitator is on the Guide Sheet.

9. As the process unfolds, keep notes about individual and group behavior that contributes to inter-group cooperation or conflict, or how people/groups manage conflict.

10. Besides the actual experience of working through the simulation, the most important part of the exercise is the debriefing, or discussion after the eighth

round. For this part, ask everyone to sit in one large circle so they can see each other. Allow a couple of minutes for spontaneous remarks and any other person-to-person comments. Now guide the discussion along these points:

A.   Who won, if anyone?

B.   What was the objective of the simulation?

C.   Why did groups cooperate or turn against each other? (Do not allow the participants to blame the facilitator for any inter-group conflict that might have occurred. Each person is responsible for their own behavior. At most, the facilitator only invited participants to develop group cohesiveness by placing them into groups, separating them, and asking them to give themselves a name. Groups were invited to send representatives to meet with each other <u>before</u> certain rounds. The literal meaning of this invitation is for the representatives to meet at any time!) Conflict is inevitable in groups. Conflict can be helpful and productive as well as destructive. How to manage conflict for good is the point.

D.   Why did groups tend to follow the rules when such following tended to be harmful to inter-group cooperation? Is there ever a time in real life when we should not "follow the rules?"

E.   What skills and attitudes do people need in order to cooperate?

11. Keep the group talking only long enough for those needing to express their anger to talk through that anger, and for the group to learn about small group behavior as it relates to inter-group cooperation and the productive management of conflict.

COMMUNITY DILEMMA GUIDE SHEET

Each group has 2 cards. One card is marked "A" and the other "B". One card will be used on each trial.

Scoring: If all groups hold up an "A" card, each group will receive three (3) positive points.

If all groups turn in a "B" card, each group will receive three (3) negative points.

If "A" and "B" cards are mixed on any trial, all groups turning in "A" cards will receive five (5) negative points, and all groups turning in "B" cards will receive five (5) positive points.

The object of "Community Dilemma" is to score the maximum number of positive points. Group scores will be posted where they will be visible to all participants.

Groups will have five (5) minutes between trials to decide which card (A" or "B") they wish to play.

TRIAL NUMBER:

1. -

2. -

3. -   (Scores on this trial are doubled)

Before Trial No. 4, each group may send a representative to meet with other group representatives for five (5) minutes.

4. -   (Regular scoring)

5. -   (Regular scoring)

6. -   (Scores for this trial are tripled)

Before   Trial   No.   7,   groups   may   again   send
representatives to meet together for five (5) minutes.

7. -   (Regular scoring)

8. -   (Scores for this trial are quadrupled)

FINAL SCORE:_____

DIRECTIONS FOR USE OF THE INSTRUMENT

"Translating Needs to Design Considerations"

Designing an educational facility begins with the needs of the potential learners. From here the planners can proceed to determining ways to meet these needs, and then to the required physical features needed in the design of the facility.

Research has revealed the general psychological and sociological needs of everyone. These needs have already been listed on this form. This was done to encourage planners to give thought to those needs that are usually overlooked when designing an educational facility.

The first step in designing a facility is determining client needs. The second step is to determine just how these needs are to be met--programs, special design features, or maybe the use of existing facilities. If special design features or using an existing facility will meet the needs, then planners can jump directly from needs to design. But if programs are to be used to meet the needs, then thought must be given to the kind of program needed before the design can be considered since different programs will require different physical features; such as rooms, hallways, lighting, storage cabinets, entryways, etc.

The form in this appendix can be used to determine the activities and related design required in order to meet the needs of learners, of any age. Use a separate form for each age group to be served by the facility.

The same process can be used when other needs have been identified. Simply use the same form but write in the discovered needs of the community in place of the general needs already listed on the form.

TRANSLATING NEEDS TO DESIGN CONSIDERATIONS

NEED	ACTIVITIES	DESIGN
Security		
Belonging		
Individual differences		
Similarities in groups		
Multi-stimuli effect on retention of learning		

NEED	ACTIVITIES	DESIGN
Effect of emotion on learning		
Varying attention spans		
Transfer of learning		

BUILDING ENERGY SURVEY

Equipment needed for this survey:
1. Light meter with readings in foot-candles
2. Thermometer

I. Look At The Facility From The Outside

Draw an outline of the facility in the space below. If the facility is composed of more than one building, pick one that contains many different units (classrooms, offices, kitchen, etc.). Be sure to place the facility in relation to North on the compass.

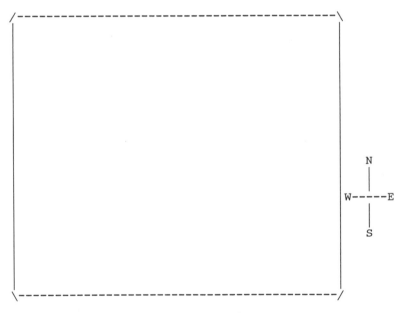

School Outline

"Building Energy Survey" based upon information from *Energy Conservation Manual*, Florida Department of Education, 1981, and *SEED*, Tenneco, Inc.

II Lighting

2. List any rooms where the lights appear too bright as measured by foot-candle meter: _____

    List any areas where lights appear too dim as measured by foot-candle meter: _____

3. Are the light switches located for easy use? _____

    Can the lights near windows be turned off? _____

4. Are the following clean?

    Windows _____

    Light Fixtures _____

    Skylights _____

III Cafeteria/Kitchen

Is heat producing equipment located next to cooling equipment? _____

IV Exhaust Fans

1. How are most exhaust fans controlled? _____

2. Can outside ventilation air dampers be closed? ____

    Are dampers working properly? _____

V Hot Water For Washing

1. What is the temperature of the hot water as it comes from the tap in:

Rest rooms	____ °F	Should be 105 °F
Cafeteria/Kitchen	____ °F	Should be 105 °F
Dishwasher	____ °F	Should be 140 °F

2. Do any faucets drip? _____ Where? _____

3. Are hot water heaters located close to use areas?

VI   Heating/Cooling System

1. Do the thermostats read/control the room tempera-
    ture accurately? _____

2. Are the thermostats well placed? _____(Should be
    about 5' from floor, away from heat or cool air,
    etc.)
                                                       o
3. What is the night thermostat setting? _____ F
                                                       o
4. What are the day settings of thermostats? _____ F

5. Can windows be opened to let in cooler, outside
    air?____

VII Putting It All Together

1. After surveying the school and answering the above
    questions, it is time to look at what you have
    discovered.

    A. List good energy management practices that you
       have observed:

B. List places you observed energy being wasted. State a possible solution for each item observed.

Energy Problem	Solution

INDEX

adults, 14, 31, 72
associationism, 26, 27, 28, 29
automated office/classroom, 58

Bruner, 26, 29
building design, 19, 25

children, 5, 7, 29, 30
choices, 24, 25
cognitive-field theory, 26, 27, 28, 29
Community Education, 10
community needs, 5, 11, 18, 71, (See Ch. 3)
computer floor, 64
computers, 28, 46, 47, 66, 67, (See Ch. 6)

Dennison, 26, 29
Dewey, 26, 29

education, 6, 7
Educational Facilities Laboratories, 42, 49, 69, 73
educational facility, 2, 8, 9, 13, 33, 40, 42, 43, 46, 50
educational philosophy, 11, 12, 14, 19, 20, 23, 25, 26
Elder Americans, 14, 32
energy, 16, 72, (See Ch. 4)
essentialism, 14, 21
existentialism, 14, 21
experiences, 5, 6, 19, 24, 26, 27

form follows function, 4, 9
funding sources, 40

Great Books, 23

Halon, 62

idealism, 21

Kohl, 26, 29
Kozol, 26, 29

learner-centered, 27
learning styles, 19, 20, 26
learning theory, 14, 19, 20
library services, 5

Marian Wilson, 42

needs, 1, 5, 8, 11, 15, 33, 53, 58, (See Ch. 3)

Pavlov, 26, 29
perennialism, 14, 21
philosophy of life continuum, 21
planning, 5, 8, 9, 11, 33, 50, 58, (See Ch. 1)
planning team, 12
pragmatism, 14, 21
progressivism, 14, 21
Pulgram
  William L, 67

Realism, 21
recreational services, 5

Schiamberg
  Lawrence B., 18
school facilities, 9
schools, 5, 6, 8, 20, 50
sense mechanism, 22, 24
Shirley Neill, 42
Skinner, 26, 29
smart building, 16
Soldatis
  Stephen, 57
Stonis
  Richard E. 47

teaching style, 19, 20, 26
technology, 16, (See Ch. 6)
The Educative Community, 7
Thorndike, 26, 29
traditional classroom, 27

vandalism, 16, (See Ch. 5)

Watson, 26, 29

Young
  George, 57
youth, 14, 35

Ziesel
  John, 57